101 Ways to Make **Learning** *Active* **Beyond the Classroom**

Elaine Biech

WILEY

Cover Design and Illustrations: Faceout Studio

This book is printed on acid-free paper.

Published by John Wiley & Sons, Inc., Hoboken, New Jersey
Published simultaneously in Canada

For general information about our other products and services, please contact our Customer Care Department within the United States at (800) 762-2974, outside the United States at (317) 572-3993 or fax (317) 572-4002.

Wiley publishes in a variety of print and electronic formats and by print-on-demand. Some material included with standard print versions of this book may not be included in e-books or in print-on-demand. If this book refers to media such as a CD or DVD that is not included in the version you purchased, you may download this material at http://booksupport.wiley.com. For more information about Wiley products, visit www.wiley.com.

Library of Congress Cataloging-in-Publication Data is on file.

9781118971987 (pbk)
9781118972007 (ePDF)
9781118971994 (epub)

Printed in the United States of America

10 9 8 7 6 5 4 3 2 1

CONTENTS

TECHNOLOGY TACTICS 97

Blended Solutions 99

e-Learning Tools 108

m-Learning 128

Social Learning 141

For free Active Training tips and tools, please visit www.wiley.com/go/activetraining and use the password **professional.**

ACKNOWLEDGMENTS

All authors list people to whom they are grateful, but this is a volume that never would have occurred without the pioneers in learning and development (L&D) who push us to be the best that we can be. Look carefully at the contributors' names at the end of the activities. They are the ones, our generous colleagues, who willingly shared their best activities so that all of us may benefit. A humble thank you to all of you. You motivate me.

Of the contributors, a special thank you to everyone who tweeted, texted, emailed, and called their colleagues; contributed extra activities; volunteered to help; and were involved in 101 other ways: Wendy Axelrod, Jane Bozarth, Peter Garber, Barbara Glacel, Catherine Lombardozzi, Karen Lawson, Lynne Lazaroff, Renie McClay, David Powell, Kella Price, Tracy Tagliati, Shannon Tipton, Amy Tolbert. Thanks for your contributions and for going "beyond" in order to make learning active.

This volume draws heavily upon what I've learned from the professionals I call the "e-learning elite" and the other industry experts who continue to encourage us through their research, their writings, their admonishments, and their brilliance. Without these people, we would not be where we are in guiding others to develop in the best and most natural ways: Clark Aldrich, Jon Aleckson, Michael Allen, Jane Bozarth, Ruth Clark, Jenny Dearborn, Julie Dirksen, Jane Hart, Jennifer Hofmann, Bill Horton, Cindy Huggett, Karl Kapp, Elliott Masie, Clark Quinn, Patti Shank, Thiagi, Karie Willyerd, and others.

Thanks to my husband Dan, who created masterpieces in the kitchen to sustain me through all of those long hours of writing: cinnamon chip scones, brandied onion soup, tarragon turkey salad, cherry glazed pork chops, portabella parmesan, and stuffed acorn squash. Mmmmmmm.

Thank you to everyone at Wiley who makes me look good: Matt Davis for reviving the series, production editor Chaitanya Mella, and editor Donna Conte.

INTRODUCTION: GETTING THE MOST FROM THIS RESOURCE

T alent developers of the world, this book was written for you. Our job is to give learners an experience that makes them leave with increased competence, confidence, and commitment. Developing people ensures our organizations have the ability to achieve their visions in a "VUCA" world. The term "VUCA" has been around for almost 20 years. Some of you may have heard the term before. VUCA stands for volatile, uncertain, complex, and ambiguous—terms that reflect an increasingly unstable and rapidly changing business world—the world in which we all work today.

As the people who guide the development of employees, we have a critical role to play in supporting the talent that deals with the VUCA world. The ability to find rare or unique talent in many specialized occupations is becoming increasingly important for organizational success, yet fewer and fewer people possess the skills required. Once the needed talent is found, how do you attract these people to your organization and keep them there? Now, before you scream "That's not my job," think about this: Can specialized talent be developed, and, if so, how? What developmental experiences are needed to grow such talent? It is your job. And ensuring that the development is exciting, practical, timely, and encourages talent to stay is also your job.

You are developing the capability for your organization's future—technical and professional skills. The pace of changes in technology accelerates each year, creating even more demand for highly educated people. Imagine the skills that will be needed in the future for things such as electric cars, new sources of energy, cyber-security, changes in government regulations, mobile computing applications, or the customization of services. Few organizations have the "capability"—the skills and knowledge for any of these or a host of other science, technology, engineering, or math careers (commonly called STEM).

There is lots of chatter about new technology and delivery systems. Your job is to find the right mix of coaching, mentoring, stretch assignments, rotational assignments, and training interventions to meet the job requirements of today and of the future. Gamification, the application of game-playing elements to nongame environments like the workplace, will continue to grow as organizations think about ways to engage their employees, assess skills, and attract talent. In addition, utilizing point systems, badges, leaderboards, and other competitive tactics to encourage desirable behaviors—such as employee health and wellness, training and development, and performance—is likely to increase. Organizations are transitioning from using gamification as a tactic into using it as a strategy, for example, using it to discover underlying business problems.

There is a new emphasis on experiential learning. Most of us know that experiential learning is effective, yet few organizations get the full benefit of this learning. Research at the Center for Creative Leadership (CCL) and the University of North Carolina shows that companies that want to develop a bench strength within their talent pool can increase the impact of development by helping employees learn from experience.

"Less is more" is one of the themes that cycles throughout conferences and conversations. As practitioners, we need to find the least amount of content that our learners need. The Internet is filled with information. We are overwhelmed with data. There is no shortage of information. What our learners need right now is just the right amount. Just as Goldilocks was looking for not too soft, not too hard, but just right, so we need to find not too much, not too little—but just the right amount for our learners. This book will help you do just that.

Few of us rely on only virtual or only classroom delivery. The activities in this text are written with that in mind. However, as you read the activities, you will easily see that they can all be adapted to many situations.

How This Book Is Organized

Top 10 Lists

You will find top tips from cover to cover. Literally! *The 101 Active Learning* book series has always started with 20 "Top 10" lists. This text does also. But it goes *beyond*—like its title. This book *ends* with a "Top 10" list. The end of this book is really the beginning of what's to come. David Powell, a futurist at CCL, shares what he believes learning will be like in the not-too-distant future with "10 Ways to Think about Learning in the Future." It is an intriguing list and one that requires a special spot. This provocative list is a great way to end the book. You will find this bonus list located between "Active Learning Idea 101" and the "Additional Reading" list.

101 Ways beyond the Classroom

The 101 techniques described in this text are divided into five sections. Each is described here to help you know where to find the technique that will be most beneficial. Note that there is crossover from one topic to another. So, just because you don't find something in one area, check another area. For example, an activity using Twitter might be found under "e-Learning tools," "Social Learning," "Technology in the Classroom," or "Online Learning Activities."

Online Learning

The section "Online Learning" delivers ideas and tools to create an exciting and practical virtual learning experience. Although the activities are designed for an online experience, each of them can be used in other settings.

- Online Openings: First contacts create a lasting impression. The first 10 minutes of any initial meeting between two people lays the groundwork for almost all assumptions and decisions about the ensuing relationship. This is true with the opening of your online session.

- Online Closings: Closings need as much attention as openings. A well-delivered closing incorporates a review, ensures that expectations have been met, confirms the transfer of learning to the workplace, and offers an appropriate send-off with a positive message.

- Online Learning Activities: Many trainers forget that they need to conduct online learning in the same way they do face-to-face learning. You can't throw adult learning principles out the door just because your learners are not in the room with you.

- Online Asynchronous Learning: Learners are able to complete asynchronous learning modules at their convenience. Interaction is still expected in these sessions; however, the interaction refers to the interface between the learner and the instructional methods.

- Unique Online Situations: These activities offer you a variety of ways in which learning can occur but may not be thought of as "developmental." You will find a strategy for learning about global needs of an organization, an online orientation, and a strategy to use to facilitate a team-building session (or any other topic) as a facilitator from afar.

Technology Tactics

Technology has opened exciting doors for learning and development in the past couple of years. Experiment with technology and discover new ways to engage your learners and deliver content in creative and memorable ways.

- Blended Solutions: Everything can fit into this category, but that does not make it blended learning. Just because you have a video, an asynchronous activity, and a classroom module does not make it "blended." Rather, "blended" means that you have chosen the best delivery methodologies to match specific objectives.

- e-Learning Tools: Breakouts, chat rooms, document sharing, polling, raised hand, whiteboards, annotation tools—these are some among many options that you have in online courses. Have you also used a meter poll, course map, Pinterest, Evernote, Poll Everywhere, or Twitter? This section presents a broad variety of tools that you can use in many situations.

- m-Learning: Think of m-learning as a miniature data point—perhaps a skill check, producing a quick connection with your learners. It must be concise, encouraging a response from your learners. It must be easy to understand, since the learners may be distracted. Ideally, it should offer just-in-time support.

- Social Learning: Social learning allows trainers to extend learning between formal training events. Using blogs, wikis, community spaces, Google Wave, Skype, YouTube, Twitter, and other social media tools for learning will maximize an organization's investment in learning.

- Technology in the Classroom: Learners bring their own tools in the form of smartphones, tablets, and laptops. Take advantage of these whenever you can. They provide multiple options for you to collect needs assessment information, survey participants, communicate messages via words or pictures (or both), and follow up later.

Learn from Many

Learning comes from many different directions and various people. Help your learners seek out other options by directing them toward mentors or peer learning groups. Help supervisors understand the critical job they have in coaching and teaching their employees, and help them find team experiences that lead to learning.

- Learning on a Team: Individuals may use cross-functional teams as an opportunity for development in large organizations. Teams are created to solve an organizational problem or to implement a process that spans the breadth of the organization and requires representation from many departments.

- My Mentor and Me: A mentoring partnership is an agreement between two people who share experiences and expertise to facilitate personal and professional growth. Mentoring provides an approach for less experienced employees to learn and hone skills that will make them more effective.

- Put Me in Coach: Most Fortune 500 companies hire coaches, both internal and external, to support their workforce. Most organizations also expect managers to coach their employees to be better at their jobs. Your job may be to help managers understand this role.

- Peer-to-Peer Learning: Providing personal and professional support between colleagues is often quite informal. These learning ideas may provide the impetus to encourage more options or enhance what is already occurring.

Learning on the Job

Everyone learns on the job. Whether you help yourself, receive assignments from your supervisor, learn from experiences, tap into the Internet, ask a colleague, or join a professional association, every experience that you have and encourage your learners to have benefits both the individual and the organization.

- Help Yourself: Self-directed learning appeals to all of us because we prefer to learn on our own and because it is self-paced. The flexibility allows us to learn when and where we want. This supports most of our natural learning desires.

- Informal Learning: The unofficial, impromptu, unscheduled way most people learn to do their jobs is responsible for 70 to 80 percent of all learning. We need to create an organizational culture that supports informal learning.

- Learn from Experience: Designing experiential learning activities to fit into classroom activities ensures learners practice skills. Bringing the real world into the classroom gives learners skills that are required to solve today's problems. Finding ways to take the entire learning group to the site is even better.

- On-the-Job Assignments: Supervisors have many tools at their disposal: rotational assignments, stretch assignments, project-based assignments, and others. Supervisors decide which learning developmental assignments will be most beneficial for each employee. As an L&D professional, you may need to help supervisors define this important role.

Learning beyond the Workplace

Learning doesn't stop when learners leave the workplace. In fact, it may just begin. As an L&D professional, you may need to help learners see the value in various opportunities outside the organization. You may also need to help them see the importance of taking responsibility for their continued learning.

- Learning Outside the Organization: You have teaching options, books to read, association meetings to attend, and people to meet. There are endless things you can do and learn about as long as you keep your eyes open and your options in focus.

- Do Well by Doing Good: Providing time and talent by volunteering is a way to learn new skills and give something back at the same time. Volunteering comes in many roles and sizes. Volunteers may have skills that they can share with others, or it may be a learning experience for them. Volunteering may occur within the same skill set and profession or may be something completely different.

Activity Design

Each of the 101 strategies is arranged in a similar format, making it easy for you to go directly to the activity that you need. Five elements describe each of the 101 activities:

Overview: A statement about the purpose of the strategy and the setting and situation in which it is appropriate.

Participants: The number of participants that are appropriate for the strategy and, in some cases, a definition of the type or level of employee that benefits the most from that strategy.

Procedure: Step-by-step instructions about how to use the strategy and things to remember to make it successful. In many cases, the debriefing questions are built into the procedure.

Variations: Suggested alternatives for ways to use the strategy.

Case Examples: Situations in which the strategy or examples of templates are used to help you visualize how the activity can be successful.

Whether you use the 10 tips list or the 101 strategies, they serve to build a range of "active learning" methods and offer tools to design and inspire active learning beyond the classroom.

200 Tips to Make Training Active and Learning Successful

Active learning beyond the classroom requires that you be aware of a myriad of details. I've continued the 101 Activity Books' tradition of opening with 200 tips that address many of these details. The tips cover everything from opening to closing a virtual learning session. You'll find ideas for engaging virtual learners and using annotation tools. There are tips for using breakout rooms, QR codes, polling, and Twitter in both physical and virtual classrooms. The tips will help you get started with using gamification, social media, and shooting a video for a learning session.

Have you been asked to lead a virtual team? Conduct virtual coaching? Check into m-learning for your company? These new 20 Top 10 lists, totaling over 200 training tips, summarize best practices and ideas on how to address some of the issues and challenges that you face. We are fortunate to have tapped into some of the best trainers in the world for these tips to make your life easier. And there is a bonus. Starting on page 297 David Powell of the Center for Creative Leadership (CCL) shares "10 Ways to Think About Learning in the Future." What an exciting way to end this book!

You may have heard of some of these tips and may already have used many of them. If you have others, we would love to hear from you and would post them on the book's website along with those listed here. The organized lists provide ideas in a flash for some of the questions that you may have.

Top 10 Lists

1 10 Tips for Successfully Implementing a Virtual Learning Platform

Kevin Costner was told in *Field of Dreams,* "Build it, and they will come." This mind-set may work for an Iowa corn farmer and a magical baseball team, but it does NOT work for a new learning system. To meet and exceed business objectives for a virtual learning program, it is important to deploy these tips with the virtual learning platform. The experience will be like a great baseball game with the crowd going wild. If you choose to ignore some of these essential steps, you will find yourself sitting on an empty bench looking at a corn field.

1. **Effective communication.** If the target audience does not know about the new learning system, they will not participate, and the desired results will not be realized. During communication, highlight why the new learning system is good for the target audience. Communicate about the online learning system with references on related websites, in newsletters, in email campaigns, on LinkedIn, on Twitter, and so on. Use physical media to highlight the availability of training (getting-started cards, posters, mouse pads, table tents in conference rooms, etc.).

2. **Set and measure goals.** Have obtainable and measurable goals for the online learning center (e.g., 1,000 new users by March 25; 5,000 users by April 20; and 3,000 completed courses by July 20). Measure and communicate the progress on a monthly basis.

3. **Access and ease of use.** Create easy access to the training (minimize barriers). A rule of thumb is that a user should be able to find and access a specific learning object within two mouse clicks from logging in. Enable easy visibility for learners to see the courses they need to take as well as completed courses.

4. **Substantial and meaningful content.** The learning site needs to provide relevant and engaging content. A new course or updated content should be available on a regular basis. Take this opportunity to communicate additional material to all learners.

5. **Think multiplatform.** Learners should be able to access training from their PC, tablet, and mobile device through multiple browser types. Insure the training is tested to work across browsers on multiple platforms.

Should you also consider a need for learners to be able to access via wearables (e.g., Google Glasses, the Apple watch, or others)?

6. **Leverage search engine optimization (SEO) to promote your website.** If the training is for external audiences, effective SEO helps users find and access the new training system through organic or paid searches. Optimizing a virtual classroom may require changes in content and HTML coding in order to improve search engine indexing.

7. **Use website analytics to optimize learning site performance.** Website analytics (like Google Analytics) help firms realize important updates that need to be made based on web page statistics. By using website analytics, firms can improve the performance of a virtual training platform by making changes to site navigation, organization, and content. Reviewing analytics will provide insight into usage trends around web browser usage, operating system usage, along with key data around times of access, the path of learners, and the region where training occurs.

8. **Secondary support.** Connect the online training with in-person training, national meetings, and webinars. Obtain senior leadership support and communicate results.

9. **Incentivize and promote engagement.** Highlight participation success. Think about a contest to jump-start the program. Highlight performance success based upon learning participation. Respond immediately to feedback or suggestions.

10. **Encourage feedback from learning.** Collect feedback in a systematic way via ratings and comments. Respond to feedback from learners in a timely and instructive manner.

Ideas from Charlie Gillette, Knowledge Anywhere, Inc.

2 10 Ideas to Create a Prewebinar Checklist

Many things can occur during a webinar over which you may have no control. You do, however, have control over the time prior to the session while you are engaged in setting it up. Create a checklist that will help you remember all of the things that you want to do to either prevent problems or to be prepared if a problem occurs during the session.

1. **Set up an "away-message" and log in at least 30 minutes prior to the session.** Ensure that you use your "away-message" in your email that includes the webinar link and dial-in information. Participants will automatically have the information needed to join your webinar so that you will not be distracted while you are setting up or starting your meeting.

2. **Log in on an extra computer.** Use a second computer and log in as a participant so that you can see what participants see.

3. **Create a memory stick and script backup.** Save your presentation on a memory stick in case you need to use a different computer at the last moment. Also, script what you will say/do so that you have a guide to follow. It's easy to get off track, especially if you experience technical difficulties.

4. **Plan to wear a headset and plug into a landline phone.** Wear a headset, preferably wireless, so that you can move about as you facilitate the session. This will project more energy in your voice. Use a landline phone for best audio results and be sure to have an Internet connection with a high bandwidth. Wi-Fi connections can vary, and you may become disconnected from the meeting.

5. **Expect differences in platforms.** Recognize that some formatting, animations, or slide transitions created in your slide program may not work with your webinar platform. Also, what works in one platform may not work in another.

6. **Close your email.** Reduce your distractions and avoid an embarrassing situation by closing down your email and instant message notifications.

7. **Script your session with a partner.** Tag-team with another facilitator. Switching voices and personalities is a good way to give yourself time to handle the technological aspects of facilitating online, and you and your

partner's personal banter will keep the audience engaged. Always use a script—with a partner or not—to keep you focused.

8. **Mute participants.** While you are presenting content, mute your audience to reduce background noise.

9. **Plan to record your session.** Recording your session allows participants to go back and key in on topics of interest. It also provides you a way to critique yourself and make improvements for the next go-round. Were there technical difficulties? Did you pause too frequently? In what parts of the session did the conversation lag? Did you say "umm" too many times?

10. **Insert a greeting slide.** Insert a slide at the beginning of your sessions with a picture of you as the host(s) so that the participants can relate to the person behind the voice(s). Go beyond the typical headshot and post pictures that show you in action—perhaps conducting a session in front of a group or even at your desk, replete with headset and computer screen. If you work with the group often, change your picture and start including pictures that show what you do outside of work, too: working in your garden, riding your horse, practicing Pilates, baking a cake, taking in a ballgame, ice skating, or whatever makes you, you.

Ideas from Tracy Tagliati, Learning and Development Consultant; Sharon Wingron, Wings of Success LLC; and Christi Gilchrist, CLG Consulting.

3 10 Slides to Organize Your Virtual Learning

When you deliver training in a virtual classroom, add a few slides to help you communicate clearly with participants. This will help you maintain your focus and organization. Here is a list of slides you can use for your training session:

1. **Facilitator slide.** Photos, names, titles, and locations of the facilitating team.

2. **Participant slide.** Photos, names, titles, and locations of participants.

3. **Interactive features slide.** Instructions on how to interact using the features of the virtual classroom (e.g., chat, raise hand, whiteboard tools) with a screen shot of each feature.

4. **Audio slide.** Description of how the audio works (one-way or two-way audio) and how the teleconference works.

5. **Agenda slide.** Show the order and timing of topics and break times. Insert this slide between sections throughout your training as you conclude a topic and start a new one.

6. **Materials slide.** If you sent materials to participants prior to the session, show a photo of the materials and describe what materials participants need and how they will be used. For example, show an image of the participant workbook and then describe what the participants should do next.

7. **Exercise instructions slide.** For each exercise, create a slide with clear instructions describing the exercise, how long it will last, which interactive features will be used, and any materials needed to complete the exercise.

8. **Transition slide.** This slide signals the transition to a new topic, a new activity, or a new facilitator.

9. **Break slide.** This slide indicates that the class is on a break and shows the time when the break ends.

10. **Concluding slide.** This slide indicates that the class has concluded. Include your contact information or website here, if appropriate.

Ideas from Darlene Christopher, author, *The Successful Virtual Classroom.*

4   10 Tips for Opening an Interactive Online Training Session

An engaging virtual training session begins from the moment participants join in. Set the stage for interactivity right from the start!

1. **Begin early.** Invite learners to join the session 10 minutes early so that they are ready to begin at the start time and in order to resolve any technical issues.

2. **Say "hello."** Greet each learner by name when they join in to make them immediately feel welcome.

3. **Engage them upon connection.** Engage learners with an activity, such as a poll question, as soon as they connect.

4. **Display the logistics.** Post a rolling slide show to inform learners about administrative items so that you don't need to spend time reviewing logistics at the start.

5. **Tell them about the tools.** Help learners get comfortable with the platform tools one at a time by inviting them to click and type on screen.

6. **Play music.** Play upbeat music to set an engaging tone.

7. **Show your face.** Turn on your webcam to say "Hello" and invite participants to do the same, even if you don't plan to use it throughout the session.

8. **Clarify what's ahead.** Set expectations by letting learners know that this will be an interactive session.

9. **Remove diversions.** Ask learners to remove surrounding distractions in their work space and to let you know once they have done this step.

10. **Chat early.** Invite learners to connect with each other via the chat feature, to form relationships, and to help them realize they are in a virtual "room" with others.

Ideas from Cindy Huggett, CPLP, Cindy Huggett Consulting.

5 | 10 Webinar Warm-Ups

You may have encouraged participants to join your virtual classroom early. What can they do if they have logged on and everything is working well? Lots! Here are a few ideas.

1. Brain teasers. Show a continuous series of brain teasers.

2. Video. Show a brief video clip that illustrates a concept from your program.

3. Discussion question. Post a discussion question and show instructions on how to use the chat feature.

4. Survey. Post two or three survey questions, and give instructions on how to "vote." Remember to show the survey results when you begin the webinar.

5. Whiteboard response. Post the whiteboard with a standard quadrant grid and show instructions for how to use the arrow feature. Pose a question and let participants use the arrow feature to display their answer. Example: "How long have you been a supervisor?"

Over 6 years	4 to 6 years
1 to 3 years	New and eager to learn

6. Cartoons. Show a series of cartoons related to your topic. Be sure you have obtained permission from the author. If all of your participants are in the same industry, the cartoons could all relate to that one industry.

7. Quotes. Show a continuous series of quotes related to the topic.

8. Fast draw. Show a "Fast Draw" story depicting a concept from your program.

9. Foundation. Show a series of slides reviewing the foundational concepts that precede your program.

10. Surprising facts. Show a series of interesting or surprising facts, such as, "Did you know...?"

Ideas from Jo Lynn Feinstein, EdD CPLP, DaVita—HealthCare Partners.

6   10 Ways to Engage Virtual Learners

Have you had times when you were facilitating a webinar and no matter what you tried, you simply could not get a response from your learners? Expect engagement and participation—otherwise, why are they called "participants"? Here's a list of great ideas from colleagues for ways to engage virtual learners. How do you do all of this and still keep your sanity? Provide behind-the-scenes support. Prepare alternative ways in which participants may reach you if they are having difficulty (via email, text, chat box). Work with a producer or a partner; take turns providing behind-the-scenes support as needed.

1. **A strong introduction.** Online courses have the reputation of experiencing high truancy rates as the courses progress. Some of this can be curtailed by ensuring that you start strong. In typical face-to-face classes, trainers often spend the first meeting allowing participants to tell their fellow classmates a bit about themselves. This practice is just as important as reviewing the course agenda and should be maintained in the online setting as well. As the first assignment, have participants submit a post to the group outlining their interests as related to the course and outside the course as well.

2. **Face time.** The best way to facilitate introductions is through a video. A majority of participants will have at their disposal the capability to record and upload a short video introduction, likely via their smartphones. The value of seeing one another's faces and hearing each other's voices, although it may not be the primary mode of communication throughout the rest of the session, is invaluable. This practice initiates a sense of community learning, no matter the physical location of each participant and, when repeated throughout the duration of course, maintains that sense of community.

3. **Foster communication.** Do not hope that online discussion will blossom as it normally would in a physical classroom; ensure that it does blossom by setting clear guidelines and allowing opportunities for it to happen. As the facilitator, you should not talk the entire time. Give participants avenues to chat with one another, discuss ideas, and ask questions of each other. This allows them to benefit from the group's experience and make connections. If the class uses posts, establish minimum requirements for how and when participants

are expected to contribute their thoughts about and reactions to assignments, including a minimum number of responses that must be made to other participants' posts, in order to facilitate a dialogue.

4. **Surprise, you've been called on.** Start with a roster of all participants' names, locations, emails, and cell phone numbers. Alert all participants that they will be called upon randomly to answer questions, make a comment, and provide a point of learning. All must stay alert and pay attention. You can use this like an energizer tool. Ask participants to disclose something about themselves to the group. This can be done at different times throughout the training session. You might say, for example, "Minneapolis, James—tell us something about yourself and about a current event from Minneapolis." In a small group, put participants' photos or names on a slide. Use the pointer to indicate who should speak next. As a rule of thumb, provide an opportunity for participants to respond to a question or participate in an activity every fifth slide. Vary how you ask participants to respond so that they don't become complacent.

   ◆ Give me a green check mark if you have finished reading page 14 or if you agree with this, or a red "X" if you need more time or don't agree.

   ◆ If you are okay with this, give me a smiley face.

   ◆ Can you chat what you think of this idea?

   ◆ Can one of you raise your hand and give me an example of a situation like this that might have happened to you?

   ◆ Pose a polling question, ask participants to elaborate in a chat box, and then call on someone to unmute his or her phone and expand on his or her response.

5. **Foster learning between participants.** Your engagement will help ensure that participants continue to check in with the ongoing discussions even after they have completed their participation requirements. But feel free to make explicit your expectation that participants follow the discussion even if they have nothing more to add at that time. Part of the advantage of the in-person learning experience is the opportunity to hear and consider the contributions of others, whose insights may be just as valuable as the trainer's. This benefit can be lost

in the online setting if participants check out of the discussion once they have fulfilled their minimum required posts.

6. **It's my turn.** Give separate small groups responsibility for some part of the content: the opening, the review of topics or debriefing of the learning, "how to remember" the content, action steps, and the close. They will stay engaged if they are truly a part of the agenda. Get involved. Give each participant in the training a separate book or portion of the agenda—one that is peripherally related to the training or for which the participant can become the subject matter experts (SME) on the topic to be addressed. So, for example, if the training is on influencing others, find books or articles that mention that topic. Then call on participants or ask them to comment as to what their books say about the topic. Ask SMEs for comments in their areas of expertise.

7. **Make it personal.** Always have a smile in your voice and an energetic tone, and make personal connections with participants right away. Keep a list of participants who have signed onto the training so that you can welcome them by name. Refer to them by name if they have questions. Send meeting materials, handouts, and assorted props in advance to each participating group. Boxes may be opened at a signal from you so that all groups see the information for the first time together. Add a surprise, for example a noisemaker, to be used for celebrations of right answers and mini contests.

8. **Engage mentally.** Check for participants' understanding of the material. Pause periodically to give them time to think. Polling the participants is an excellent way to check for understanding after a point has been introduced. By leaving time for questions at the end of the session, you can also check for their understanding. Challenge the participants to find one new idea during the webinar. If you have the option, use multiple presenters. The change in voices will keep the interest level up. Keep the participants' attention with frequent slide movement: transition, zoom in, annotate, or highlight slides every 30 seconds.

9. **It's the end.** End on time; if you don't, you'll lose them anyway. Bring closure to the session by asking participants to raise their hand and share the one most important takeaway from the session. Watch to see who responds; if someone is not responding, consider calling on that person to share a key item.

10. Between session engagement. The session ends, but your engagement should not. You want your participants to continue to be engaged in the topic. As the trainer, you can post readings, videos, and discussion questions ahead of time. Stay current with discussions on the discussion board in order to make connections, further dialogue, encourage and praise good work, and pivot the course of the conversations as necessary. Expect participants to apply their new skills between sessions and ask them to report at the next session. Use projects or between-session assignments to build engagement as well. Assign team tasks and projects. Encourage virtual teams to use tools such as Skype, Hipchat, or Slack for real-time communication and a video that the team can use for a meeting.

Ideas from Linda Bedinger, The AthenA Group, LLC; Cynthia Clay, NetSpeed Learning Solutions; Ashley Glacel, PhD Candidate, University of Maryland; Barbara Greenstein, Human Resource Prescriptions, LLC; Tracy Tagliati, Learning and Development Consultant; and Charlotte S. Waisman, The AthenA Group, LLC.

7 | 10 Tips for Using Annotation Tools

Using the annotation tools available will help to keep your participants engaged. Too many trainers think of annotation tools as only what they can do: draw, point, highlight, or write. But real engagement comes when you turn the annotation tools over to the participants, allowing and even encouraging them to draw, point, highlight, or write. When participants contribute to the training session by using the annotation tools, they can't answer emails or do anything else. They are truly mentally and physically engaged.

1. **Play time.** Allow participants to play with the annotation tools when you first start the training session so that they feel more comfortable using them. Get them physically involved early to increase the odds of their active participation. With a small enough group, have them use the text tool to write their first name in a color of their choice on-screen. Check the names against the participant roster. Then check with those whose name you do not see to learn if they need help. A side benefit is that it sends a message that you are attending to who is participating and who is not.

2. **Alternative roll call.** Familiarize your participants with the annotation tools by taking a roll call. Prepare the whiteboard ahead of time by writing in a list of the participants and then ask them to put a check mark next to their name. Additionally, ask them to put an "X" next to the names of the other participants they know.

3. **How are you doing?** At the start of each session, ask everyone to change the status of their feedback status icons. Or, ask a question that can be answered by the icon, "How's your workload today?" or "How much do you remember from last week's session?" or "How easy was it to implement what we discussed last time?" Be prepared to respond if comments aren't all "happy faces." Perhaps you can offer to check in with those who need support after the session. At the very least, ask participants to change their status to a particular feedback mode and back again to ensure that they know how to change it.

4. Raise your hand. Familiarize your participants with the hand-raising tool by asking questions related to the topic: "Raise your hand if you are a first-time manager."

5. Let's chat. Familiarize your participants with the chat box by asking questions related to the topic: "Type in the chat box the one word that describes how you feel as a manager." Leave the chat functionality enabled. Use it early yourself to ask an open-ended question to which you expect responses. Ask questions that elicit short responses. When asking a new question that requires a chat box response, type in a marker, for example "Question #3." That way, you will know where to stop when you are reviewing all of the responses in the chat box.

6. Large groups can chat, too. Divide a large group of participants into smaller groups when posing a question for the chat box. An easy way to do this is by instructing them to do the following: "If the last digit of your telephone number is 1, 2, or 3, type in the chat box." Keep the other participants engaged by instructing them to read the responses of the others and to choose the best one. Then say, "If the last digit of you telephone number is 4 or 0, read through the responses and choose the best one."

7. Whiteboards for anonymity. If your webinar platform has a whiteboard option, you may want to use it in order to elicit responses about provocative or sensitive issues rather than have the participants type their responses in the chat box. The whiteboard allows for anonymous responses, whereas the chat box identifies the author of each response. Participants may be more willing to share their thoughts and insights when they know their responses are anonymous. Another option is to draw lines on the whiteboard to divide the board into sections so that the participants don't type over each other. You can say, "If your last name begins with A–E, type in this area." Some webinar platforms have multiple whiteboards; if so, divide the participants into groups and assign each group a whiteboard on which to respond. You can say something like, "If you live in Alaska or Wisconsin, type your response on whiteboard number 1."

8. **Turn it over to them.** Encourage participants to use the annotation tools whenever they desire. You can make your own rules, for example, "Give me a check mark if you agree with the content," or "Give me an 'X' if you have a question." Sometimes it might be distracting to use the annotation tools, or they might draw silly pictures to entertain themselves. Consider this: If they are using the annotation tools, they aren't answering emails.

9. **Call attention.** Use the annotation and drawing tools available to you to call attention to items on a slide in the same way you would for items on a flipchart or a whiteboard in a conference room.

10. **Learn to draw.** Few trainers use the drawing tools. Practice drawing even the simplest sketch to change the pace a bit. Design activities that will put the drawing tools in your participants' hands as well.

Ideas from Tracy Tagliati, Learning and Development Consultant.

8 10 Tips for Using Breakout Rooms in a Virtual Classroom

The use of breakout rooms is equally as effective in the live virtual environment as in the physical classroom. You will find that these tips are consistent with what you would do if you were in a physical classroom. Breakout sessions and small-group activities require more prework and organization in a virtual setting. And, of course, you require technical skills and knowledge to manage the activities as smoothly in a virtual classroom as you would if participants were physically present. Once you've conquered them, you will find breakout rooms in a virtual setting to be identical to those in a physical setting.

1. **Prepare.** Be sure that the breakout room is prepared in advance.

2. **Directions.** Put a slide with instructions in each breakout room in advance.

3. **Whiteboards.** Instruct participants on how to take notes using a whiteboard.

4. **Moderators.** Identify one person in each group to act as moderator and to give permission, if necessary.

5. **Groups.** Arrange participants in breakout rooms or allow them to move themselves into rooms electronically. This may take some practice or instruction.

6. **Circulate.** Move from room to room to ensure that everyone understands the task and is working toward the end product.

7. **Timing.** Use a timer and send an electronic announcement prior to having participants return to the main room. Consider sending reminder messages also, such as, "You have used half of your time" or "You have two minutes to wrap things up."

8. **Completion.** Consider using a system to return all participants to the main room simultaneously, rather than encouraging them to return separately. It is efficient and much easier than having to move from room to room. The drawback is that it is abrupt.

9. **Results.** Carefully bring the groups' notes on whiteboards back to the main room. This is like having them return with the flipchart that they created.

10. **Debriefing.** Use a similar debriefing process and questions as you would if the session were held in a physical setting.

Ideas from David Bush, PhD, Villanova University.

9   10 Tips for Using QR Codes in Learning

A Quick Response (Quick Response) code is a digital image that can be scanned without the beam of light needed to scan barcodes at the supermarket. It's used in advertising and marketing for smartphone users. You may have seen QR codes on flyers, subway posters, brochures, and even cereal boxes. They are often accompanied with a message that says, "For more information, scan this code." They can be scanned using one of the many free QR scanner apps available for smartphones and tablets. When you scan the code, you'll be taken directly to a website. QR codes are easy to make and can quickly change your normal routine. One use for QR codes that is easy to appreciate is that it eliminates the frustration of typing long web addresses and takes your participants directly to the website.

1. **Provide a QR code tutorial.** Be sure to send all participants a tutorial on how to use QR codes.

2. **Gather data.** Take participants to a poll or a learning survey to participate.

3. **What's the date?** QR codes can be used to create a calendar item or event. It can facilitate adding a learning event to participants' electronic calendars.

4. **No more long web addresses.** Provide participants with links directly to content, such as a video, a website, or an article.

5. **Save time and trees.** Using QR codes can reduce paper usage and provide participants with an online version of learning materials that can be downloaded.

6. **Stay in touch.** Offer a QR code with your contact information to make you available for web chatting or a phone call.

7. **Share resources.** Participants may request additional reading or resources. Create a reading list and provide a QR code to participants to access the list.

8. **Follow-up support.** If participants need additional review on a concept, use a QR code to link them to a tutorial or additional resource to support their learning.

9. **QR code scavenger hunt.** Add some fun to your session. Create a scavenger hunt using a QR code to introduce material or to present content. You can do this in a virtual or a physical classroom.

10. **Preparation before your session.** Provide prework materials for a learning session using a QR code. You can also use a QR code to direct participants to a needs assessment in order to collect information about their experience, goals for the training, and level of knowledge on the subject matter.

Ideas from Dr. Kella Price, SPHR, CPLP, Price Consulting Group.

10   10 Polling Tips for Virtual Classrooms

The polling feature in a virtual classroom allows the facilitator to post questions to participants and show poll results, either in real time or after all responses have been received. Polling can reveal interesting information about the participants' background or level of knowledge, as well as opinions on your session's topic. Ensure that polling goes smoothly with a few guidelines:

1. **Use concise language.** Check the language of both the poll question and the answer set to make your poll clear and to the point so that participants will quickly respond.

2. **Avoid acronyms.** Spell out acronyms to avoid confusion.

3. **Avoid compound questions.** Don't ask a question about two items (e.g., "Was the reading assignment interesting and relevant?") if you offer only one option (yes or no).

4. **Avoid leading or biased questions.** A leading question prompts the participants to respond in a particular way, for example, "Why do you prefer virtual classroom training for further skill development?"

5. **Use mutually exclusive answers.** Ensure that your answer sets don't have overlapping responses. For example, if you ask the participants where they are right now and the choice of responses is, "At work, at home, at a hotel," how would someone respond who is working in a home office?

6. **Include a "don't know" or "not applicable" option.** When appropriate, include a "don't know" or "not applicable" option in your answer set to ensure that everyone will be able to respond to the poll.

7. **Use a poll reminder slide.** Insert a slide to remind the facilitating team when the poll should be conducted.

8. **Rehearse with your polls.** Practice the timing of when you will launch the poll, how you will comment on poll responses, and when you will close the poll.

9. **Decide how you will share the poll results.** Most virtual classroom tools provide facilitators with options to share the poll results in real time or to broadcast the results at a specific time chosen by the facilitator.

10. **Don't overdo it.** Constant polling can annoy participants. Make sure to use a variety of interactive techniques to engage participants.

Ideas from Darlene Christopher, author, *The Successful Virtual Classroom*.

11 | 10 Phrases to Regain Virtual Participants' Attention

Many participants will multitask while attending webinars. The phrases listed below will help you regain their attention. In addition, you may wish to say nothing at all. Remaining silent for a few moments will also work to regain your participants' attention.

1. Periodically ask a question related to the topic: "What do you think is...?"

2. "If you have one takeaway from today's webinar, it should be...."

3. "Please read the key points on this slide."

4. "A word of caution..." or "I should warn you...."

5. "What most people find astonishing about this is...." or "Believe it or not...."

6. "Here's something interesting...." or "Even better,...."

7. "Has this ever happened to you...?"

8. "Let me repeat this important point...."

9. "If you are still not convinced, listen to this...." or "Here's the secret...."

10. "You are going to love this...."

Ideas from Tracy Tagliati, Learning and Development Consultant.

12 10 Tips for Using Twitter for Ongoing Learning

If your learners actively use a messaging tool like Twitter, you might piggyback on that practice by opening an account that learners can follow regarding a specific topic. Here are 10 things that you can do and post to remind learners of their knowledge or skill.

1. **All may not be equal.** Some participants may not be Twitter users, so make it equitable for everyone. Send participants a tutorial on how to use Twitter. Share your Twitter username or handle with all participants and include it on course materials. Collect participant usernames and create a list in Twitter of the users in order to direct the content to them.

2. **Encourage teamwork.** Communicate the hashtag that you will use for the course. Encourage learners to follow each other, not just the program's feed. Create Questions within the hashtag for participants to answer. Encourage them to ask questions, too.

3. **Set a date.** Organize a #twitterchat for a specific date and time. Send links to prereading, if appropriate. Capture results and post them for learners to view if they miss the chat.

4. **Send links and quotes.** Curate recent online articles or videos and send links. Send inspirational quotes that are related to the same information or skills. For example, if the content is about change, you can Google "change quotes" for hundreds of choices.

5. **Start a meme.** Start a #hashtag meme (keep it positive). For example, ask participants to share their best employee recognition ideas this week via #HighFive.

6. **Reinforce others' involvement.** Retweet some of your learner's posts as encouragement and to prompt them to follow each other.

7. **Tweet a "minilecture."** Post a "minilecture," which is a series of 5–15 posts that make a specific point.

8. **Promote follow-up.** Inform participants about follow-up programs and enrichment exercises.

9. **Introduce experts.** Invite learners to follow specific people who are thought leaders on the subject.

10. **Introduce surprise.** Occasionally, share unrelated posts to inject personality into the tweet stream (e.g., vacation pictures, funny links, commentary on TV shows). Obviously, make sure that all the program tweets are "safe for work."

Ideas from Catherine Lombardozzi (@L4LP) and Dr. Kella Price, SPHR, CPLP, Price Consulting Group.

13 | 10 Tips to Get Started with Games and Gamification

Game-based learning and gamification are both common phrases in training and development. Both have staunch support from the profession, and both are considered innovative methods to help learners develop. You may hear them used interchangeably, but they are not the same. Games are the ideal learning environment, with built-in permission to fail and built-in motivation to succeed. Game-based learning is the use of games to teach and reinforce educational objectives. According to Karl Kapp, gamification is the use of game mechanics to make learning and instruction more fun. Gamification uses "parts" of games.

1. **Embrace games.** Games are fun. Create opportunities for learners to compete against other learners. Create opportunities for them to compete against themselves or the clock. Any of these create instant engagement. Simulations and games can be a bonus to designing learning.

2. **Know your learners.** Provide game elements that suit the learners and what their intrinsic motivation for learning is. Are they competitive? Collaborative? Socially motivated? Loners? Is the game being designed for a sales staff? Project managers? If you are not sure, then provide game elements that suit every type of player.

3. **Work with stakeholders to clearly define the performance goal.** A goal can be fun to design and experience. It still must have a well-thought-out design connected to a performance goal in order to be a learning tool. The success of the game hinges on this step. Be clear about the performance goals that are required.

4. **Create the design.** Like designing a training program, creating a game is both an art and a science. Experience other games and designs to garner ideas. Read Karl Kapp's book, *The Gamification of Learning and Instruction*, to help you sort out the steps. Remember, you want the game to be motivating, reinforcing, safe for experimenting, challenging but achievable, goal oriented, and performance focused.

5. **Create a story.** If the performance goal is clear, a story will be easier to create. You can use audience analysis to create realistic situations. Identify the conflict and decision-making elements of the story.

6. **Define clear rules.** Rules must be clear and concise. Rules that are too long or too difficult will not motivate your players. Test the game to determine if more guidance needs to be added to the rules or if the rules are too complicated.

7. **Create frequent feedback.** Feedback on the job helps employees determine whether they are doing things correctly and, if not, how they can correct the behavior so that they can experience a more positive outcome. The same is true with a game. In Ruth Colvin Clark's book, *Evidence-Based Training Methods,* 2nd edition, she defines four guidelines for giving feedback: Be specific, provide instructional and intrinsic feedback, adjust frequency of feedback based on what is required, and focus on performance goals.

8. **Link the reward.** Achieving a reward for "winning" the game is not enough in the world of talent management. Knowing what to do isn't enough either. Players need to transfer their knowledge to the workplace. It is more effective to link the reward to both the game and the performance achievement.

9. **Match game strategy to learning content.** Create the right learning outcome with a careful choice of strategy. As trainers, we realize how difficult it may be to change our attitudes, values, and beliefs. However, even this is possible by selecting the right game strategy.

10. **Play games.** Games are fun, but if you seriously want to learn more about games and the role they play in learning and development, you need to play them. Go to http://tinyurl.com/gamification to learn more.

14   10 Ways to Use Social Media Tools to Support Learning

The availability of new technologies and the adoption of social media within most organizations create a unique opportunity for trainers and facilitators to support learning in an ongoing format. Social media offers a variety of tools, applications, and platforms to provide a wealth of resources and materials to support both virtual and classroom learning. Use Twitter, blogs, wikis, Facebook pages, Google Docs, YouTube, Skype, and others to expand opportunities to connect with learners formally or informally.

1. **Prior to a learning event.** Prior to a learning event, tweet short introductions, ask participants to create a short YouTube introduction, or dedicate a wiki page for participants to list their favorites (e.g., books, hobbies) or comments about the class (e.g., what they hope to learn, why they are taking it). This sets up the wiki to be used later for class projects.

2. **Between session work.** Some classes may be separated by days or even weeks. Blogs can be used to keep participants involved with the topic between sessions. Post a link to a recent article, ask for examples of what participants implemented since the last session, encourage questions or concerns, or provide a case study for participants to resolve and discuss in the next class. Tweet reminders or recommendations based on what they learned in the session.

3. **Check up after a class.** Follow up with participants after a class to support them once they return on the job by using Twitter to ask what they need, providing tips to implement new actions or a recommended reading list. One way to help learners manage the 140-character limit is to offer them a sentence stem so that they can simply complete the thought, for example, "One thing that concerns me about the new customer service policy is...."

4. **Continue participant engagement after a class.** To encourage involvement after a virtual or physical class session, ask participants to take responsibility for tweeting their successes. Use a wiki for participants to contribute to a permanent searchable record of notes or comments.

5. **Organizational change prerollout.** Communication before a major change in organizations helps employees understand what will happen. If this is done well, social media can help employees learn about their roles and what to expect. Communication can answer questions, allay fears, and dispel rumors.

6. **Postchange rollouts.** After a major change, employees may uncover aspects of the change that they have not anticipated. Help employees learn by sharing their successes, answering questions, or celebrating accomplishments of those who have achieved certain milestones of the rollout. A social infrastructure in place allows the organization to capture new ideas, flawed thinking, workarounds that employees are using, and problems that employees experience. This organizational learning is valuable to make quick policy or procedural adjustments.

7. **Just-in-time.** The real test of whether a skill was learned is in the implementation of it in the workplace. Knowing when a learner will be faced with implementation can be supported with just-in-time suggestions and reminders. Tweeting "Good luck" can be done before a big meeting or presentation. Providing a checklist as a reminder before a day of interviews or project reviews will be appreciated.

8. **Improve communication.** Check into current technology to enhance communication. For example, use Skype or Hipchat for real-time communication and for showing a video during a meeting. Check out lesser-known technology such as Slack, which offers a real-time messaging, archiving, and search tool that facilitates better communication within a team.

9. **Certification and recertification.** Many organizations require compliance certification for employees and for technical topics. Social media tools can support this by keeping employees abreast with policy or requirement changes; creating discussion forums for staying on top of policies; or curating questions, concerns, and information for fast retrieval. At some point in the future, organizations may certify based on contributions to posts that demonstrate knowledge.

10. **Start a book club.** Set up a Twitter account and establish a schedule for reading each chapter of a book. On the scheduled date, tweet a question, asking things like "What key point was important to your job?" "What surprised you?" "What would not work here?" or other provocative questions. Use a blog or wiki for longer commentaries.

Ideas from Jane Bozarth, author, *Social Media for Trainers* and *Better Than Bullet Points*.

15 | 10 Tips to Be Successful with m-Learning

Learning can be accessed from the palm of your hand. What could be better? M-learning, short for "mobile learning," can be accessed on smartphones, tablets, laptops, and some wearables. M-learning allows you to pair a tiny but critical (either time or importance) data point with a skill check, giving you a quick connection with your learners. This accomplishes several things. It provides learners with content, allows them to provide you with an update, and keeps the relationship between the two of you active. But be careful; m-learning is not e-learning on a miniature screen. The user, the purpose, and the environment are different.

1. **Think small.** To ensure readability, imagine the smallest device that will be used for the content, such as a smartphone, and then design for it. When the content is transferred to a larger device, such as a tablet, the content will also look good.

2. **Think concise.** Content should be delivered in five minutes or even shorter time capsules. M-learning is not repurposed e-learning. It must be redesigned. Only include what is absolutely necessary. Mobile learners expect to acquire information quickly and easily, so break the content into small bites that can be digested rapidly.

3. **Think engaging.** Create content that hooks learners from the first contact. The content must be engaging and attention grabbing. Determine why learners would want or need the content.

4. **Encourage a response.** Integrate social learning strategies into the content to make it interactive. Well-designed content encourages a response from the user. The response needs to be easy and short.

5. **Plan for diversions in the environment.** Content should be straightforward and easy to understand, since the user will not likely be in a distraction-free environment when reviewing the content.

6. **Create just-in-time support.** Ideally, m-learning offers performance support or knowledge required just-in-time, like an updated policy, a job aid, or a short communication skill.

7. **Find the right development tool.** Ask colleagues and others about their favorite development tool. Finding the one that works best for you is important. For example "gomo" by Epic Learning allows you to create a multidevice learning file, and "gomo" configures the information for all devices.

8. **Get them emotionally involved.** You can boost learners' involvement by increasing their emotional connection to the content. This may occur by offering rewards or real-life examples that will help learners relate to the content.

9. **Present videos.** One of the best learning tools at your disposal is a video. Script it concisely and edit it freely. If the video is over four minutes long, consider dividing it into segments. The ideal video for a small device is from two to five minutes in length. Look into a private YouTube channel for videos to reduce interface issues.

10. **Clarify expectations.** Everything will not look good on all mobile devices. At times, you may have a file that requires using a tablet or a laptop. If that's the case, establish clear expectations with your learners; inform them up front in the explanation.

16   10 Tips for Shooting a Video

Why use a slide to demonstrate how to load a forklift when you can show a video? New technology makes creating a video much cheaper and shooting it much easier. This does not mean that you can throw caution to the wind and ignore preparation and planning. With planning you can create powerful videos for your learners. Jonathan Halls believes that if you do not spend about 40 percent of your production time on planning, there is a chance you will end up repairing mistakes or changing something that you forgot.

1. **Get familiar with your equipment.** Make sure you know how to focus the camera and adjust the exposure, how the mike works and where it plugs in, how to monitor the audio, how to adjust the tripod, and so on. Know the various automatic exposure (AE) settings on your camera and be sure to select one that's well suited to your lighting and type of video.

2. **Ensure you have all needed supplies.** Do you have a battery for the mike and a backup? Is the camera's battery pack charged, and do you have an extra battery pack or a way of plugging it in? Do you need a teleprompter or outline for your talent to reference?

3. **Stake out your location.** Do you know exactly where you'll shoot the video? Do you have lights available and the appropriate set-up materials, or do you know if natural lighting will work (maybe try a sample take at the same time of day you'll be shooting to check levels, shadows, etc.). Do you know if it will be quiet at the time you will shoot, or do you need to put a sign on the door or other markers to avoid people outside making noise? Is there ambient noise (e.g., air conditioner, heater, traffic noise) that needs to be eliminated? Are there *nonswiveling* chairs available? What will the backdrop look like? If you're using a white sheet or a green screen, does it need to be ironed? If you will be using a natural backdrop, do you need to eliminate distracting clutter (e.g., signs, messiness)? Do you want to move something into the shot for balance (like a plant off to the side)? Is the background complementary but not distracting? *Note:* Never shoot right up against a wall or with a bright light source (like a window) directly behind the subject.

4. **Prepare your talent.** Send the talent that you will be using guidelines on appropriate dress, glasses, colors, or other important information that will

show them in their best light. This makes them feel comfortable that you have thought of everything.

5. **Find a helper.** Get someone who can monitor the camera and sound during the shoot. They don't need to have any technical expertise, but they can save you a lot of time if your mike starts acting up or people drift out of the frame, rather than discovering problems after everything is wrapped up.

6. **Double-check the mike.** Bad sound will ruin the shoot. Make sure that you know how to position the mike and how to set the levels to avoid distortion (level is set too high) or excessive noise (level is set too low).

   - Turn off the automatic gain control (AGC) on the mike, since it will dip up and down depending on who is speaking. Manually adjust the gain so that it averages around −20db. It's okay for it to occasionally hit −12 or −6 for occasional peaks in volume. Peaks of 0 or higher will cause distortion.

   - For best results, use a portable audio recorder. A camcorder's built-in mike usually produces poor-quality sound.

   - If using lavalier (clip-on) mikes, make sure the mike cable is hidden (can go behind shirts, etc. with the transmitter box in a back pocket). If talent has long hair make sure that the mike is low enough that hair won't hit the mike when people are talking.

   - Plug headphones into the mike's output so that your helper can monitor the audio and alert you immediately to any problems.

   - Turn off anything in the room that can beep: cell phones, computers, and so on. Put up signs outside the door that you need quiet.

   - Record some room tone. Before starting, have your mike(s) record nothing but the sound in the room (8–10 seconds is plenty). This is useful in sound editing to eliminate any room noise by sampling the sound without talking above it.

7. **Shooting a single subject for best results.**

   - Frame your subject on the right or left one-third of the frame (rule of thirds). Do a midshot (i.e., cut them just above or below the belt line on the bottom and leave some headroom on the top). If the content has more emotion behind it, you may want to go for a tighter shot, where you frame just at or below where a necktie knot would appear. Keep in mind that you can tighten the shot later in editing but you can't pull back, so use this approach with caution. If a subject will use visual aids, think about how to position the visual aids so that your talent doesn't turn away from the camera (or suggest editing in slides or other visuals later, unless the subject needs to interact directly with the visual).

- Have the subjects look to the interviewer on the opposite side across the frame, just a bit off center (not too far). If they are lecturing, you can have them speak directly to camera.

- Position your subject's eyes about one-third of the way down from the top of the frame.

- Have your subject talk a bit to be sure that you can see their hands and that their body doesn't move out of the frame.

- If you are in doubt, go a bit wider than necessary (i.e., showing more of their body and surroundings.) When shooting in high-definition, it's possible to reframe a shot in editing by tightening the shot. However, if parts of the body are cut off or the subject is too close to the edge of the frame, there's nothing you can do since they have not been captured on the video.

8. Shooting a two-person interview offers options.

- Have the interviewer and interviewee sit next to each other in a tight "V" so that the camera can see both sets of eyes. It can be challenging to have the two people interact but still be facing "mostly" front. (It's okay to see some profile on occasion, but the eye quickly tires of it.) A good alternative is to separate them a bit physically across a table or other central object, with one person appearing in the left third and the other in the right third. Now they can talk to each other, but they are also facing (mostly) toward the camera. Also, the person being interviewed can practice addressing the camera more than he or she is addressing the interviewer.

- If you have two cameras, you can train one on each subject from an angle so that you get each properly framed as described earlier—they can be edited together later.

- With a single camera, you can first train the camera exclusively on the interviewee, framing him or her properly (both eyes, left or right third, and so forth). Then the interviewee can leave, and the interviewer "re-asks" the questions after the camera has been repositioned.

9. **Leave space at the beginning and end.** Don't start talking the second the camera starts working. Avoid having people say, "Good job" or talking the second the take ends. Start the camera, let it roll for a few seconds with the talent in place, and then begin. At the end, hold the position for 5–10 seconds before shutting off the camera or allowing people to speak.

10. **Plan retakes.** For retakes, think in terms of paragraphs, not sentences. It's very difficult to edit in a single sentence retake. An entire thought, example, or story can usually be adjusted more easily.

Ideas from Ron Rabin, Center for Creative Leadership.

17   10 Tips for Virtual Coaching

Executive coaching is a relationship-based exchange between a coach and a learner, with relationships best formed through spending time together. But as organizations become global and time becomes a scarce resource, the use of virtual means of communication becomes more important. To increase the effectiveness of virtual coaching, here are some tips to remember.

1. **Select the best platform.** Research the various platforms for virtual coaching, practice using your preferred platform, and be ready to substitute methodology on the fly when a technical problem arises.

2. **100 percent attention.** Agree on how to focus during the virtual session and not to be distracted by intrusions, such as incoming emails or interruptions that may not be obvious in the virtual setting.

3. **Timely responses.** If the virtual contact is nonsynchronous, agree to a time period in which a message will be answered.

4. **Clear agreements.** Typical coaching agreements must be more explicit in virtual coaching to include ethics, confidentiality, boundaries, logistics, methods, and times of contact.

5. **Personality inventory.** In a new virtual coaching relationship, it is helpful to start with a personality inventory, such as the Myers Briggs Type Indicator, in order to get to know each other and both of your preferences.

6. **Use a camera.** Relationship building is enhanced when you are using a platform that includes a camera so that body language and facial expressions can be seen.

7. **Trust is critical.** Trust building may require more self-disclosure about personal information, background, and experience. Begin and end each session with informal comments to ease stress and open the dialogue in a personal and holistic setting.

8. **Take notes.** Listen deeply and take notes on the conversation in order to track the flow of the conversation. If you are on-camera, tell the learner that when you are not looking into the camera, it is because you are taking notes.

9. **Match communication to the issue.** The more complicated the issue is to be discussed, the better it is to use a synchronous form of virtual communication. The more routine it is, the more likely that asynchronous communication will suffice.

10. **Review more often.** Cocreate the coaching journey by frequently sharing what is working and what is not working in the virtual relationship. Use frequent process checks during the conversation. Share mental models. If misunderstanding or conflict occurs, back up and talk about assumptions.

Ideas from Barbara Pate Glacel, PhD, The Glacel Group.

18   10 Tips for Virtual Teamwork

Virtual teams exist in dispersed locations, whether they are across town or across continents. Team members depend on each other to accomplish their shared work, and they must focus constantly on how to cross the boundaries of time, space, and shared goals.

1. **Start with a face-to-face meeting.** Find time early in the work process to get together face-to-face. If the team stays together for a length of time, meet face-to-face on a regular basis. Take a photo of the team at this first meeting.

2. **Personalize.** Learn something personal about each member of the team so that you can exchange a minimum of small talk when you begin an interaction.

3. **Exchange photos.** Post photographs of the teammates near your computer screen or next to the telephone so that you can envision your teammates when you are interacting with them. Better yet, use video conferencing to see everyone whenever possible.

4. **Implement process checks.** Use frequent process checks to assess how the relationship is growing and how the work is progressing.

5. **Communicate regularly.** Keep communication flowing even if there is nothing in your work together that is pressing.

6. **Solve issues immediately.** When something seems amiss, rely on more personal communication rather than less. Solve the problem by face-to-face interaction if possible; if it's not possible, work through the options in this order: videoconference, telephone conference, personal email, electronic meeting place.

7. **Practice email etiquette.** When you are using electronic communication, be attuned to heightened emotions. If you feel frustrated or angry, take a process time-out before sending a response.

8. **Share responsibility.** Each team member must share responsibility to get the team on track if anything about the virtual nature of the session—or anything else—is getting in the way of meeting the goal. Be aware that team members have other priorities and obligations that you may be interrupting.

Because you cannot see the team members, you do not know what their activities are at the moment you need them.

9. **Be flexible.** Share expertise and build virtual networks to include suppliers, customers, and even competitors who may be linked in a virtual strategic alliance.

10. **Build commitment and responsibility.** Match the right skills to each and every requirement, and ensure that team members share ownership and accountability for the job and a sense of pride in the team's accomplishment.

Ideas from Barbara Pate Glacel, PhD, The Glacel Group.

19 10 Tips for Leaders as Teachers

Today's leaders cope with information explosion, continuous and rapid change, globalization, and uncertainty. This climate requires that leaders pass on knowledge, information, and philosophy to those who are working for or with them. They must consciously discuss their strategy, vision, and values to others in the organization. In short, leaders must develop their employees.

1. **Confirm and communicate.** Spend time confirming what you believe in and assuring yourself that you are aligned with the company's strategy, and what values you want demonstrated. Then take every opportunity to tell others about your beliefs, strategy, and values.

2. **Tell stories.** Tell stories about the history of the organization, the profession, and the principles that you want demonstrated.

3. **Create group discussion opportunities.** Meet in small groups with colleagues and employees to discuss the business and where it is headed.

4. **Practice all communication modes.** Spread knowledge by every means available—written, spoken, behavior—and by high-tech and low-tech media to reach those both near and far.

5. **Consistency is key.** Make your message consistent over time and consistent with that of other leaders in the organization.

6. **State why.** Explain "why" as well as "what."

7. **Model what you expect.** Lead by example so that your behavior becomes the mentor and coach.

8. **Go beyond the organization.** Use activities outside the organization, such as community service, as a classroom for teaching.

9. **Develop yourself.** Develop your teaching skills through your own leadership development activities. Practice learning from others so that the teaching is a mutual exercise.

10. **Discuss decisions.** Mentor and coach employees by reflecting on why decisions are made by management, the impact of management's decisions, and their fit with the company's strategy.

Ideas from Barbara Pate Glacel, PhD, The Glacel Group.

20 10 Tips and Options for Training in Virtual Reality Environments

3-D immersive environments provide us with vast options, because the technology blurs the line between the simulated world and the real world. In 3-D immersive and interactive environments, learners view objects in true 3-D without relying on imagination. Good 3-D immersive environments keep learners involved and interested.

1. **The environment's design.** A virtual world stands as a metaphor. Pick a guiding metaphor that supports the work to be accomplished. As an example, coaching someone is like embarking on a journey of discovery. Given this metaphor, you might build a mountain that you both can "climb" and "reach the summit" together. If you are teaching powerful people to have reciprocal empathy, you can construct a world, like in the movie *Honey, I Shrunk the Kids,* in which all everyday objects are huge and the avatars are small. Use this as the backdrop for a discussion of power, impact, and leadership.

2. **The environment's purpose.** When designing a virtual world, you must continually ask yourself, "What value does doing the task in a virtual world have over doing the task in the 'real' world?" If speaking on the phone (also a virtual reality) provides equal impact value, then working in a 3-D immersive environment adds an unnecessary layer of complication. Don't complicate things.

3. **Managing attention, part 1.** Remember, you are creating a virtual "visual" environment. Make the environment visually interesting. Give learners things to look at and objects to engage with. Ask them to "find" something. Give them tasks to do. If you don't do this, then the work is reduced to disembodied voices talking on a headset. In this case, a phone call would serve better.

4. **Skeuomorphism.** When building a virtual training space, there is no need to mirror the physical world or to obey the laws of physics. Since avatars never get tired, they do not need to sit. If they do not need to sit, why build a room with chairs?

5. **Use open sightlines.** When you are building a virtual world, remember that people, in reality, will be looking at a small monitor, like looking through a

window. Create a psychological sense of openness by building environments with open sightlines. If you want to hang images in a virtual museum, you can build transparent walls. Let your imagination run away with you.

6. **Sound.** You control the sound. The sound dynamics of rooms do not apply. You can create open environments with tightly controlled sound. You can control whether a speaker is heard by all, regardless of location, or by only those within a specific location. Remember to design the sound for the task. You can design two open, unwalled, virtual "breakout rooms" right next to each other, where only the people within each "room" can hear each other.

7. **Teaching movement and camera control. Keep it simple.** All instruction about movement and camera control should be embedded in the task at hand. For example, the first time the participants need to turn left to look at something is when you teach them how to turn. Never give them more instruction than is necessary for the current task at hand.

8. **Managing attention, part 2.** If the hands are engaged, so is your virtual participant. Remember, while people can see and hear in the virtual world, they are looking and acting through a computer keyboard. You cannot know what they are really doing in the "real" world by looking at their avatar. Give them an instruction to look at something or to move someplace, and they will be required to attend and engage through using the keyboard.

9. **Reviewing virtual documents.** As a corollary to number 8, give participants as much action control over the environment as possible. As an example, if you are reviewing an assessment or other document together, have the virtual participant advance slides or turn the pages of a PDF file. Remember, if the hands are engaged, so is the participant.

10. **Recovering what is lost.** Whether you are working with one person, a team, or multiple teams, allow "in-world" virtual leaders the ability to transport team members who get separated from the group back to the leader's location. This is a powerful and necessary control, as people can (and do) get lost.

Ideas from David Powell, Center for Creative Leadership.

Online Learning

Online Openings

First contacts create a lasting impression. The first 10 minutes of any initial meeting between two people lays the groundwork for almost all assumptions and decisions about the ensuing relationship. This is true with the opening of your online session. The opening of your virtual online training session should accomplish the same things that an in-person opening accomplishes. It should include an initial assessment of your learners' skill level; establish session expectations and norms; identify who is in the group; promote interest and enthusiasm; and put participants at ease.

1   Picture Me

Overview

Use this strategy to assist in creating connections among participants virtually and increasing engagement. It promotes interaction and goodwill toward each other and reinforces the concept of "I like these people, and we're in this together."

Participants

Up to 12 people in a webinar or virtual meeting

Procedure

1. Prior to a webinar or virtual meeting, ask participants to email you a photo of their favorite vacation spot (pick one topic or leave it open), of them as a baby, of their pet, of their kids, or they can pick their own topic that relates to the meeting's content.

2. Also ask them to send a *brief* description (one sentence preferably) of the content of the photo and/or why they chose that photo.

3. Post the photos between content throughout the meeting as a way to break up the concepts and give people's brains a "refresher." Don't post them all at the same time.

4. Thank everyone at the end of the meeting for participating by sending in photos.

5. End with a collage slide of all of the photos.

Variations

- If participants know each other, you can ask them to guess at the end of the training session whose picture belonged to whom.

- Give a prize to whoever guesses the most correctly or whoever can remember all of the different photos and the people. If you tell them at the beginning you'll be doing this, it will spur people on to pay attention to the whole virtual learning from start to finish.

- If the meeting is long enough for breaks, have the photos rotate during that time.

Case Example

In a training session about virtual team building, begin with a slide that says "Picture Your Team." Post the first photo and caption. After debriefing each virtual team topic or activity, post a new slide and caption. This activity will sustain interest and provide a break during content-rich e-learning.

Contributed by Rob Fletcher, Quixote Consulting.

2   You Intro Me; I Intro You

Overview

Paired participants introduce each other.

Participants

Any number, but time could be an issue if the group is large; on the other hand, if the group will meet together more than once, the time investment for future engagement is worth it

Procedure

1. Pair participants using chat rooms or breakout rooms.

2. Assign two to four short bites of information that each should learn about the other. Allow about six minutes.

3. Bring the group together and ask participants to introduce their partners.

Variations

- This can easily be done in a classroom setting.

- To save some time, pair participants before the session and have them meet their partners prior to the start.

Case Example

Virtual team members, located in three different countries, were each paired with someone prior to the session. They were to connect and learn three pieces of information about their partners.

- Name, location, and job role

- What excites them about being on the virtual team

- The aspects of teamwork about which they want to learn more

At the first meeting, members were given time to introduce each other. Pairs were given a task to complete before the next meeting a week away that explored some of the issues the team was facing.

Contributed by Patricia L. Johnson PhD, Certified Health and Wellness Coach, St. Luke's Health System.

3   Quote Me

Overview

Use this strategy as an opener to get participants thinking about the topic.

Participants

4–20 in most learning situations

Procedure

1. Prior to the session, select a number of quotations that relate to the topic. Plan on one quotation for each three to four participants. In a group of five participants or less, assign each person a different quotation.

2. Assign the quotations prior to the virtual classroom and ask each person to think about how the quotation relates to the topic and be prepared to discuss it.

3. Introduce the activity by explaining that you want to start the participants thinking about the topic.

4. Assign individuals with the same quotation to a chat room.

5. Give the subgroups 10 minutes to discuss the quotation as it relates to the topic and how they have seen the meaning of the quotation demonstrated in the workplace.

6. At the end of the designated time period, ask representatives from each subgroup to summarize the subgroup's discussion for the rest of the group.

7. Follow up with questions such as the following:

   - What was your reaction to the quotations?

   - How relevant are the quotations to the topic?

   - Which quotation had the most meaning for you? Why?

   - What was the benefit of this activity?

   - How might you draw on these quotations in your role at work?

Variations

- As an intersession assignment, participants would present their interpretations of the quotations and personal examples to the rest of the group. Interpretations could also be posted to the group's wiki or blog.

- The procedure can be used in a classroom setting to stimulate discussion or as an assignment between sessions in a multisession course. Post the quotations on flipcharts and have participants form around each flipchart.

Case Examples

1. In a session on leadership, you could do the following:

- ♦ Assign the following quotations:
  - ○ "You get the best effort from others not by lighting a fire beneath them, but by building a fire within." Bob Nelson
  - ○ "The key to successful leadership today is influence, not authority." Ken Blanchard
  - ○ "People tend to resist that which is forced upon them. People tend to support that which they help to create." Vince Pfaff
  - ○ "Before you are a leader, success is all about growing yourself. When you become a leader, success is all about growing others." Jack Welch
  - ○ "Outstanding leaders go out of their way to boost the self-esteem of their personnel. If people believe in themselves, it's amazing what they can accomplish." Sam Walton

- ♦ Ask participants to respond to the following:
  - ○ What the quotation means
  - ○ How it relates to one's success as a leader
  - ○ Cite specific examples where they have observed this principle being applied (or not applied) in their workplace

2. In a program on dealing with change, you could do the following:

- ♦ Assign the following quotations:
  - ○ "We must become the change we want to see." Mahatma Gandhi
  - ○ "It is not the strongest of the species that survive, nor the most intelligent, but the one most responsive to change." Charles Darwin

- The difficulty lies not so much in developing new ideas as in escaping from old ones." John Maynard Keynes
- "Any change is scary, and when we are scared, we use our power of fantasy to come up with scenarios of disaster." Dr. Arthur Freeman and Rose Dewolf

- Ask participants to respond to the following:
  - What the quotation means
  - How it relates to the topic of change

Contributed by Karen Lawson, Lawson Consulting Group, Inc.

4 | Using Prezi to Build Community in the Virtual Classroom

Overview

The goal of this activity is to provide learners with a chance to get to know the other learners in a new course environment. Using the multimedia presentation tool, Prezi, learners create a short presentation to post on the Learning Management System (LMS) to introduce themselves, their backgrounds, and their interests.

Participants

15–20 new learners at the beginning of an online class

Procedure

1. Develop criteria for what you would like your learners to share in their presentations. (Examples can include where the learners grew up, whether they work, a learning goal for this course, interests and activities, as well as a question for the rest of the group.)

2. Have the learners complete their virtual presentations and post a link on the LMS.

3. Set up a virtual space (wiki, discussion board, or other space) to allow the learners to respond to each learner's question of the group.

4. Provide a time line for the learners to review the presentations and to provide feedback.

5. Have the learners reflect on the process by writing a short reflection piece addressing the activity.

6. Debrief at the start of the first synchronous virtual setting, facilitating the discussion and breakouts.

   ◆ What did you learn about your fellow learners and yourself?

   ◆ How might this be helpful to your virtual learning experience?

   ◆ How is a sense of community important in the virtual learning environment?

Variations

- Create small groups (three to four learners) to work together and review each other's presentations. Depending on the size of the group, reviewing a large number of presentations can be time consuming for the learners.

- Allow learners to use different media tools to develop their introductions (Google Apps, PowerPoint, Word, or other Internet-based applications).

Case Example

For an undergraduate course that is an introduction to education, learners were asked to build the presentations around the following specific prompts:

- Give us a face to the name! Provide an image of yourself.
- Tell us about your educational background.
- What do you like to do when you aren't in school or working?
- What type of teacher do you want to be and why?
- Ask a question of the group—something you would like others to share with you.

Contributed by Rachel C. Plews, doctoral candidate, Teachers College, Columbia University.

5 | Instagram Intros

Overview

Use this strategy for virtual introductions using a photo from a phone or desktop.

Participants

Interaction is best with 50 or fewer participants

Procedure

1. In your welcome materials, send instructions on how to set up an account with Instagram and how to use hashtags (this is a great job aid). Ask participants to use a photo from their phone to introduce themselves. The photo can be of something that they love, an activity that they enjoy, or someplace that they've been.

2. If they don't have any photos on their smartphone, they can take a "selfie" with a drawing to answer the question. If they don't have a smartphone, they can use a photo from the Internet to respond to the introduction requirement.

3. Tell participants that you have posted your photo and introduction as an example.

4. Have participants upload their photo to Instagram plus a very brief introduction that connects them to the photo.

5. Encourage the group to use a hashtag to catalog their introduction by subject as well as #introduction to make it easier to find later.

6. At the start of the session, explain that the group includes all types of learners, from different areas and backgrounds. (Give examples of one to three learners.) Encourage learners to connect and reach out to each other.

Variations

- Ask the participants to submit a bio with their photo.

- If you are trying to have participants connect with others, you can ask them to find similarities with one to three other participants.

- In a smaller group setting, you can ask participants to introduce another participant.

- You can also use another social media platform, like a Facebook Group, a Google+ Community, Pinterest shared board, or LinkedIn Group.

Case Example

I recently celebrated with my kids at a church Family Night.

My bio: I have 20 years of experience in human resources, training and development, and talent management functions. As CEO of Price Consulting Group, I am a trainer and facilitator. I have four kids ages 5, 7, 10, and 15, and am married to a Marine. We live in Yuma, Arizona. #HR #introduction

Contributed by Dr. Kella Price, SPHR, CPLP, Price Consulting Group.

Online Closings

Closings need as much attention as openings with a focus on content. Don't let your time become so short that you are unable to end appropriately. A well-delivered closing may incorporate a review of the content, ensure that expectations were met, and confirm that the knowledge and skills will be transferred to the workplace; evaluation; a shared group experience; and an appropriate send-off with a positive message.

6 | Review, Remember, Relate, Recall

Overview

A closing is a quick way to summarize a learning event.

Participants

Any manageable number of participants in a virtual classroom setting

Procedure

1. Assign one of these words to each participant: *powerful, flexible, creative, fun, responsible, goal-oriented, Oh no!, sensible, important, difficult, understanding, wow, help, interesting, stimulating, easy, exciting, perform.*

2. Form participants into groups of three to four in a chat room.

3. Ask each group to create three to five summary statements about the subject of the session, using the words they were assigned.

4. Have each group report their statements.

5. Facilitate a summary using the following debriefing questions or others of your own:

   - Review: What surprised you during your review?

   - Remember: What is the most meaningful thing you will remember from this session?

   - Relate: How can you relate this content to what you need to do back on the job?

   - Recall: What is the most important thing you want to recall once you return to the workplace?

Variation

This activity may be conducted in a physical classroom using words printed on index cards. Hand one index card to each participant.

Case Example

Upon completing a communication-style workshop, a group responded with the following statements:

- Review: During our review, we were surprised that our strengths in our communication style could become our weaknesses so easily.
- Remember: We will remember to try to move into others' comfort zones.
- Relate: We need to relate communication styles to our employees' needs.
- Recall: We want to easily recall how our communication style comes across to others.

Contributed by Jean Barbazette, The Training Clinic.

7 | Make Them Stick

Overview

Use this strategy to capture how people will apply what they learn.

Participants

Any number of participants during a learning experience or team action-planning discussion

Procedure

1. Create a blank whiteboard space and ask, "How will you apply what you learn today?"

   • Variation: "What actions will you take starting tomorrow?"

   • Variation: "What new tasks do you have on your 'to-do' list?"

2. Invite participants to annotate their plans on the whiteboard. If you wish, and depending on the topic, you may designate specific areas for them to respond.

3. Provide a broad overview. This may sound like, "So far we have identified a dozen actions of how you will apply what we learned today to our daily performance, such as _____. Take a look at what others have noted. What additional actions might make a difference for you, your team, or your business? Please record your own actions or those actions that others have contributed so that you will remember."

4. Immediately after the experience, organize and type all of the actions. Email the list to all of the participants.

5. One month after the experience, redistribute the list of actions and ask participants to share "What difference did this make?" to the group. Provide an example, if possible.

Variation

You may wish to extract key action words to create a "Wordle." Distribute it to the group as a follow-up.

Case Examples

1. During a leadership development experience that is focused on coaching, you might identify specific actions such as:

   • Schedule a conversation with direct report to discuss career opportunities.

   • Use the resources provided to plan a coaching conversation, monitor progress, and foster accountability.

   • Share what difference this makes to your people and business.

2. During a technology skills review, you might identify specific actions, such as:

   • Update an Excel spreadsheet to include charts.

   • Talk to the team about using a shared Outlook calendar for scheduling organizational learning opportunities.

   • Develop a new SharePoint page for resource sharing.

   • Share what difference this makes to your people and business.

Contributed by Kimberly Seeger, MS, CPLP, Senior Talent Development Leader.

8 Choose and Choose Again

Overview

Use this strategy to review key ideas. Participants choose the best idea while reviewing key points in a presentation.

Participants

Best used for 5–30 participants

Procedure

1. After presenting content during a webinar, share a final slide that lists the key points of the presentation. (Number the key points on the slide.)

2. Ask the participants to read through the list of key points and choose the one they think is the most useful (practical, inspiring, necessary, whatever you think is the best objective).

3. Ask participants to type the number of the key idea in the chat box and then to review the chat box and identify the key point(s) selected most often.

4. Lead a discussion using these questions:

   - Why do you think the most popular key point was chosen by so many people?

   - Did you choose the most popular key point? Why or why not?

   - If you had to choose the next best key point, what would it be?

5. Ask participants to review the list again, consider what should be added to the list, and enter it in the chat box.

6. Ask the participants to review all of the additional tips in the chat box and choose the best one.

7. Debrief the activity to encourage participants to consider how the key points relate to their jobs. Questions might include:

- Which key idea will have the biggest impact if it were implemented?

- Which key idea will be the easiest (most difficult) to implement?

- Which key idea will you implement first (last)?

- What actions will you implement in the workplace as a result of this activity?

Variations

- Instead of key points, use best tips, best strategies, key actions, or other appropriate terminology.

- Show the list of key points at the beginning and ask participants to choose which one they think is the most important. After presenting the content, show the list again and ask the participants to choose the one they now think is the most important. Ask if their answer has changed. If so, why?

- If your webinar platform allows participants to annotate, ask them to put a check mark next to their choice rather than typing the number in the chat box.

Case Examples

1. In a webinar for managers on the topic of how to deliver feedback to employees, ask participants to read through the following list of key actions for providing feedback to an employee and to choose the one they think is the most important. Tell them to type the number of that key action in the chat box. Ask them to review the chat box to identify which key action was the most popular. Ask if a seventh action were added to this list, what should it be? Have them enter it in the chat box. Ask them to review all of the additional key actions in the chat box and choose the best seventh tip.

How to Provide Feedback to an Employee

- Prepare ahead of time.

- Convey your positive intent.

- Describe specifically what you have observed.

- State the impact of the behavior or the action.

- Ask the other person to respond.

- Focus the discussion on solutions.

2. In a webinar on interviewing techniques, ask participants to read through the list of tips for putting a candidate at ease and choose the one that they think is the most important. Ask them to review the chat box to identify which key action was the most popular. Ask if a sixth tip were added, what should it be? Ask them to review all of the additional tips in the chat box and choose the best sixth tip.

How to Put a Candidate at Ease during an Interview

- Be on time.

- Shake hands.

- Exchange names.

- Offer the candidate water or coffee.

- Begin with general questions.

Adapted from a Thiagi activity by Tracy Tagliati, Learning and Development Consultant.

9 Concept Challenge

Overview

A strategy that allows fun competition and a light review.

Participants

Virtual classroom of less than 20 participants

Procedure

1. At the end of the session, tell the participants that you are going to show one of the key concepts on a slide but that the letters will not be in the correct order, like the example, "SROTENM." Unmute all microphones and tell them that once they figure out the correct word, they should shout it out.

2. Show the accurate word, *MENTORS*.

3. Next, challenge them to identify several of the important things they learned about that topic or concept. Use your roster of names to call on someone if you do not get a response.

Variation

If you have a group that has more than 20 participants, use chat room and have the participants enter the name in chat. Once you see the correct word, ask them to enter several ideas that they learned about the concept.

Case Example

SROTENM	MENTORS
LAIRTUV	VIRTUAL
GGGNNAEI	ENGAGING

Online Learning Activities

Virtual classroom tools offer a core set of features and functionality. Many trainers forget that they need to conduct online learning in the same way they do face-to-face learning. You can't throw adult learning principles out the door just because your learners are not in the room with you. Screen sharing, chat rooms, drawing and pointer tools, polls, instant feedback, breakout rooms, and other tools are there for the facilitator to use to encourage interaction. Work toward finding the best way to design a virtual classroom session that truly engages participants. Practice using the facilitation techniques that work best online.

10   Using Analogies

_____ Overview _____

Good activity to use in order to introduce a topic.

Participants

Any number of participants that will be comfortable in the virtual classroom

Procedure

1. Prepare whiteboard space with three to four of the following headings:

- Designing a change effort is like ballroom dancing because....
- Designing a change effort is like building a house because....
- Designing a change effort is like sailing a ship because....
- Designing a change effort is like running a marathon because....
- Designing a change effort is like cooking a gourmet meal because....
- Designing a change effort is like planning a family reunion because....

2. Assign individuals to different places on the whiteboard. Tell them to brainstorm and enter their responses to the statement(s) in five minutes.

3. Ask groups to rotate to the next space and add new responses in the next five minutes.

4. Have groups rotate and write new responses until they have rotated through all of the statements.

5. Either have one person report back for each whiteboard space or summarize the ideas yourself.

6. Add your comments about how this relates to the session content. Transition to the next section and reference comments from this activity throughout the session.

Variation

Substitute the topic of your training for "designing a change effort."

Case Example

In a change management learning session, participants contribute the following thoughts to "designing a change effort is like building a house because...."

- Both need a solid foundation.
- Both need a blueprint.
- Both require many people with various skills.

Contributed by Jean Barbazette, "The Training Clinic," based on an activity from The Training Clinic's workshop, "Managing the Training Function."

11 Virtual Learning by Quadrants

_____ **Overview** _____

Use this strategy when you want learners to quickly analyze a scenario or case example while capturing their responses to multiple discussion questions in a virtual classroom.

Participants

4–28 participants in a virtual classroom

Procedure

1. Present a one- or two-paragraph case on a PowerPoint slide and in the participants' materials.

2. On another slide, list four discussion questions that are designed to analyze the case.

3. Have participants briefly answer the four questions in their participant guides first. Then, if using a web conference platform like Adobe Connect, open a layout with four chat pods corresponding to the four discussion questions. (Or, alternatively, create a four-quadrant grid on a slide or whiteboard, and have participants annotate their responses in the grid.)

4. Have participants enter their responses to each of the four questions in the appropriate chat pods (or on the slide/whiteboard).

5. When all quadrants have been filled, have participants read all of the comments to each discussion question.

6. Clarify and summarize with a few questions.

   ♦ What similarities and differences do you see in the responses to each of the four questions?

   ♦ What new insights do you have about this case example?

- What comment surprised you?
- How will you apply what you learned from this discussion in your work?

Variations

- To save time, divide the participants into four groups by birth month (e.g., January to March) and have each group answer one of the four questions using the chat box or annotation. Be sure to label the chat pods or the quadrants on the slide with the appropriate months.

- Select one participant for each of the four questions to unmute his/her microphone or telephone to debrief an assigned question.

Case Examples

1. For conflict resolution, present a simple scenario in which two people misunderstand each other. Ask four questions: (1) How does Person A see this situation? (2) How does Person B see this situation? (3) What should Person A do or say to demonstrate that he/she is willing to resolve the situation positively? (4) What should Person B do or say to demonstrate that he/she is willing to resolve the situation positively?

2. For building empathy, tell a story about a challenging situation you have faced in the past. Identify four typical categories of responses often given by listeners (smoothing over, judging, problem solving, and empathizing). Ask participants to give examples of each type of response in the appropriate chat pod or quadrant.

Contributed by Cynthia Clay, NetSpeed Learning Solutions.

12   Incorporate MOOC (massive open online course) Design Concepts into Your Online Design

_____ Overview _____

Augment your training—online or place-based—with these ingredients of MOOC design.

Participants

30 to 1 million participants

Procedure

1. Using a synchronous design, have everyone working on the same assignments at the same time so that learners can share what they learn with each other (this is common in a physical classroom but not so common in online classrooms).

2. Provide social tools such as discussion forums (online), group work (online or in the session), or some other way of communicating with other learners. This is a must for a MOOC-style design to work.

3. Break the training into short "absorb" activities broken up with simple "do" activities, such as Khan Academy-style short videos with basic checks on learning every five minutes or so.

4. Assign projects to learners. At the end of the training, learners should walk away with a project that represents a real (if simple) application of the course content.

5. Have learners review each other's work. The best MOOCs require anonymous peer review as a way of giving learners real human feedback on their projects. Require each learner to review four other learners' projects each week in order to receive credit for his/her own work. Provide a rubric as a guide for what to look for and make comments.

6. Gather feedback about the process with these questions:

    ◆ Were you able to answer your questions by asking other learners instead of by trying to contact the faculty?

- Were you able to absorb the videos without propping your eyelids open with toothpicks?
- Did you get useful feedback from your peers on your project?

Variations

- This could be used in a physical classroom.
- Try putting yourself on camera instead of recording your voice over the top of a slide deck. People prefer looking at other people.
- Source some of your videos from other instructors and subject matter experts, interact with other people in the videos, and toss in a few brief comic skits. A little variation in style and personality keeps things interesting and makes learners look forward to the videos.
- Employ others to answer questions in discussion forums, especially if your group is small. With fewer learners, there is less chance that the learners will provide useful answers in the forums.

Case Example

A structured project for a MOOC-influenced training on engineering standards might include these elements:

- A real application, such as designing a component of a suspension system for a car. Using a single application instead of letting learners choose their own project will make peer review and feedback more effective, because the instructor can provide the right answers.
- A four-week series of assignments that is scaffolded, moving from very simple standards to more advanced standards.
- Rubrics that learners use to anonymously review four other learners' assignments each week. Rubrics help elicit useful comments and constructive criticism, and can also generate grades.

Contributed by Andy Hicken, Web Courseworks.

13 Small-Group Data Analysis

Overview

An activity that uses actual data over two sessions to learn about data, marketing, and/or a customer segment.

Participants

Any number of participants who can organize into breakout rooms

Procedure

1. During the first session, facilitate a brief lecture about the need to target a particular marketing demographic. Invite comments about what information might be needed. Provide each participant the survey (of up to 10 multiple-choice questions) and explain their roles.

2. Between sessions, assign each participant to gather data from a specified number of individuals (one to five, depending on the size of the group and how the data will be used, if at all). Have them conduct the marketing survey. Once the data has been gathered, have them submit it to a preplanned location.

3. Export survey data into a spreadsheet before the next session. Share the spreadsheet with all of the participants.

4. During the second session, assign individuals to breakout rooms.

5. Allow 20–25 minutes for each group to analyze the results and prepare a presentation that makes a recommendation based on the data.

6. During this time, move between breakout rooms to answer questions and ensure that everyone understands the task.

7. Once the time is up, bring everyone together and ask for their conclusions and recommendations.

8. After hearing all of the participants respond to the conclusions and recommendations, ask questions such as:

- What data drove your decision?
- What data seemed incomplete or missing?
- What was the process by which you came to your recommendation?

9. Add your own conclusions and thoughts.

10. Ask, "What do you think we need to do about these results?"

Variation

You may use a prepared data set to save time and allow for a more planned debriefing.

Case Example

A retail store wanted all of its employees to understand the needs of their customers. Each employee was given three $5 coupons to award three customers who answered a five-question survey ("5 for 5"). Responses surprised most of the participants and helped them understand how they could be more helpful to their customers.

Contributed by Jennifer Hofmann, InSync Training, LLC.

14   Social Media Sharing about Implicit Bias

Overview

Colleagues take the Implicit Bias Test, which is free on the Internet, and discuss implicit bias via Facebook, email, or other social media.

Participants

Best done with less than a dozen participants, although there could be an unlimited number

Procedure

1. Complete the Harvard Implicit Bias Test at https://implicit.harvard.edu/implicit/takeatest.html. After doing this, assess who in your organization or group would be comfortable participating in a discussion based on the test.

2. Determine the best social media that should be used based on who will participate. Invite colleagues to take the Implicit Bias Test, which is free on the Internet, and discuss what they learn about implicit bias via Facebook, email, or other social media. Invite only participants you think would take the activity seriously and would be open to having a substantive conversation about it.

3. Invite participants to participate in the Harvard Implicit Bias Test. They need to go to: https://implicit.harvard.edu/implicit/takeatest.html. There is no charge to take the test, and the results are confidential. Rather than using the link, participants can search for "Harvard Implicit Bias Test." Have them go to the "Take a test" option. You may suggest that they take a specific test or that they select one or more to take. If you want them to take a specific test, name that test. Also suggest that they click on the phrase "general information about the IAT" in the "Preliminary Information discussion" and read that information.

4. Invite participants to share their learning and insights about implicit bias. Suggest that they "reply all." Say that you do not expect them to share their results. Invite them to discuss these specific questions:

   ♦ State two or three things that you learned about implicit bias from reading the general information.

   ♦ State two or three ways you believe implicit bias could impact your organization.

   ♦ How would you suggest that you address the issue of implicit bias in your organization?

5. Facilitate a social-based discussion about the participants' responses using some of these follow-up questions:

   ♦ Were your results accurate?

   ♦ Did your results surprise you?

   ♦ Did you believe the results?

   ♦ Did you decide to take additional tests? Why or why not?

   ♦ How big of an impact is implicit bias in your organization?

   ♦ What types of decisions could implicit bias impact?

   ♦ Who else should take this test?

   ♦ How should you use this test and the information about implicit bias?

Variation

Taking the test could be used as prework for a session on implicit bias or a general diversity and inclusion workshop. The questions could be discussed in the session.

Case Example

A federal government agency established a diversity counsel and used the Implicit Bias Test as a team-building activity. The participants were astounded at the things they learned about themselves. It helped them to understand the issues the agency was facing, giving them more compassion for all employees.

Contributed by Julie O'Mara, O'Mara and Associates.

15   Think-Pair-Share for Webinars

_____ **Overview** _____

During the webinar, create a teach-back session with a traditional "think-pair-share" exercise.

Participants

Assign participants into groups of two to four individuals each; you will need a participant list in advance to prepare for this activity

Procedure

1. Create groups of two to three people for each breakout session.

2. Create chat rooms in the webinar program. If chat rooms are not available, have the participants create a group chat room within the webinar chat function.

3. Have the group designate a "speaker" so that they can be prepared to give information back to the larger group.

4. Ask the speaker to be prepared to give a "Stop Doing, Start Doing, Keep Doing" takeaway to the larger group.

5. After the small group reports, ask:

   • What new idea have you gathered based on this exercise?

   • What deeper questions do you have about the topic?

Variation

Rather than having each speaker discuss the three points, create a whiteboard within the webinar program. Have three boxes labeled "Stop," "Start," "Keep" and have the groups write at least one answer to share with the group. This can be a takeaway for the participants later.

Case Example

A virtual team that was working under tight deadlines took an hour during a team meeting to work through this exercise. Some of the results included the following:

- Stop complaining.
- Start doing more check-ins.
- Keep sending updates on time.

Following the session, the facilitator turned each of the items into a short message and sent them one at a time in a tweet to all team members throughout the next two weeks.

Contributed by Shannon Tipton, Learning Rebels.

Online Asynchronous Learning

Online asynchronous learning refers to the delivery of training that does not require the learners and facilitator to be online at the same time for learning to occur. Learners are able to complete asynchronous learning modules at their convenience. Interaction is still expected in these sessions; however, the interaction refers to the interface between the learner and the instructional methods. Tools that course designers use to incorporate interaction include quizzes, tests, control of order or rate, added dimension through video, and opportunities for reflection.

16   Creating a Culture Dream Team

Overview

Having a strong brand is the lifeblood of many organizations, especially in retail, hospitality, or franchise-based industries where people create the brand experience for guests and patrons. Leaders are expected to build and foster cultures within the individual locations that support the success of the brand. Use this e-learning design approach as prework to manager or leader on-boarding. Participants will arrive with a shared vision of the culture and an aligned expectation of themselves as leaders of the brand.

Participants

Typically, general managers hired by franchise purchasers to manage a particular location or department

Procedure

1. Context: e-Learning is set within the context of the business, perhaps a top-down view featuring all of the different areas of the space. Employees are shown, as are customers, in a variety of settings in the location.

2. Challenge: On-screen, the participant receives communication from the franchise owner that his/her location performance is merely "satisfactory," but the owner expresses encouragement that the manager has what it takes to make the site's performance GREAT. The communication includes a few recent social media comments to back up the data, as well as a link to view a couple of YouTube videos created by employees in other site locations.

3. Activity: Each employee/customer in the scene represents a scenario. The participant clicks a scenario, reads a quick background about the scenario, and chooses from three to four employee actions the one that is best suited to the position/task (the one the participant believes who will live the culture and support the brand through his/her actions). This continues until all of the employees have been selected for each scene.

4. Feedback: The participant does not receive feedback until all of the employees in the scene are selected. Feedback comes in the form of performance data and social networking comments. Potentially, the participant could choose to view or watch additional culture-related material before trying again. The participant can modify the mix of employees until he/she is satisfied with the improved performance. It's okay to leave this without a 100 percent correct answer, as it will set up rich conversation during the instructor-led training.

5. Closing: A variable ending can create a great jumping-off point for the beginning of an instructor-led class, in which participants discuss who they chose and why, compare their scores, and then complete other activities that further engage the leader in the culture of the organization. Use the "tips and options" list below as a follow-up to this asynchronous activity.

Variations

• For more complex businesses, multiple scenes may be needed (strive to keep them short and interesting).

• Optionally, additional culture storytelling experiences can be included in the scenes—signs on the wall with values, links to other videos that hint at the culture, and so on to provide layered opportunities to learn more about the culture or other leaders' descriptions about creating a successful brand culture.

Case Examples

1. For a hotel brand, have general managers explore scenarios that shape the guest's experience: cleanliness of the lobby, friendliness and efficiency of the front desk staff, cleanliness of the rooms, helpfulness of housekeeping staff, qualities of department supervisors, and so on.

2. In retail settings, have store managers explore the upkeep of the store and the interactions with sales associates and customer service staff.

3. For a restaurant chain, have restaurant managers explore the quality of the different food stations, the interactions with guests at the register, and the cleanliness of the ordering area, the dining room, the restrooms, and so on.

Here are some tips and options for helping leaders foster a strong culture:

- Share many stories with everyone in the organization—YouTube videos, best practice tips, case studies.

- Encourage employees at every level to contribute to the conversation.

- Create ongoing, brief team activities that managers and supervisors conduct to explore and strengthen the culture (pep talks, huddles, quick skill practices).

- Build a system that allows peers to nominate each other for awards.

- Provide a social platform for employees to use to discuss the brand and the culture, and to share stories. Avoid making it management-driven.

- Create hiring profiles that help identify employees who will be a good "fit."

- Regularly share the performance of the business and make direct links to how service or customer experience impacts it.

- Recognize that some culture-building efforts will be less successful than others; the idea is to cast a lot of "seeds" and see which ones grow.

- Continue to offer new and fresh communications and experiences around culture, even if what you have right now is good.

- For franchise situations, make sure owners are on board with the importance of brand and brand culture so that they can provide site management with the resources and support needed to be successful.

Contributed by Dr. Michael Allen, Allen Interactions, Inc.

17 Point-Counterpoint

_____ **Overview** _____

By developing controversy and encouraging learners to play the role of "devil's advocate," the point-counterpoint strategy can engage learners in a short pseudodebate.

Participants

Large groups of learners in almost any digital learning course

Procedures

1. Select a starting statement related to a course topic to be discussed by learners (see examples below). Although controversial statements are not necessary, they can further engage learners in the activity.

2. Instruct participants that whether or not they agree with the required perspective, each posted reply must reflect the opposite perspective on the topic as the previously posted message. Provide an example or two.

3. Encourage learners to play the role of "devil's advocate" and to post responses that may not be representative of their personal perspective on the issue.

4. Participate in the forum discussions, adding point or counterpoint postings when useful for extending the activity and exploring various dimensions of the polar perspectives.

5. End the point-counterpoint activity when learners can no longer identify an alternative perspective on the forum's topic statement.

6. After all the back and forth, bring things to closure by asking summary questions. You may also wish to schedule a formal debriefing using these questions:

   - Did one perspective have a stronger position?

   - Which points (or counterpoints) most influenced your position by the end of the discussion?

   - Describe what it was like to post a counterpoint that did not represent your personal perspective.

Variations

- With minor modifications, you can use the same strategy for a synchronous (real-time) discussion.

- Sample starter statements can include the following:

  - The current role of the federal government in telecommunications is inappropriate for a free marketplace.

  - The influence of religion in education today is unconstitutional.

  - The importance of self-directed learning in distance education has decreased with the popularity of social media.

  - By testing null hypotheses, researchers create confusion and miscommunication for readers who are interpreting results.

  - The application of Deming's quality management principles continues to be useful in today's high-tech businesses.

  - Situational Leadership® tactics should be used by all managers within the company.

Case Example

Topic: "All company training should be done online."

Point: "Yes, I agree that all of our corporate training should be done online."

Counterpoint: "No, I can't learn without small group discussions, so I disagree that all training should be done online."

Point: "Online courses often include small group discussions."

Counterpoint: "Okay, we can have group discussions online, but without the nonverbal cues, it is too confusing to be effective. Learning requires one-on-one, in-person interactions."

Point: "By using acronyms and emoticons, we can make up for the missing nonverbal cues and make online discussions very effective."

Counterpoint: "Acronyms and emoticons are very limited and don't provide the necessary nuances."

Point: "Younger staff are always using technology and can easily learn without in-person interactions."

Counterpoint: "Younger staff can use technology to buy music, but they don't really learn much from online courses."

Contributed by Ryan Watkins, PhD, George Washington University, based on an activity in *75 E-learning Activities: Making Online Courses More Interactive* by R. Watkins.

18   Onboarding New Employees

Overview

This online learning strategy, which is accessible to all, acquaints new employees with the organization, its structure, key personnel, and specific required learning programs.

Participants

All new employees, their managers, and supervisors—individually or in small groups

Procedure

1. This class is set up in learning modules and requires that supervisors check with the employee after each module is completed. There is a short quiz administered after each module.

2. Class completion increases organizational understanding and helps answer questions that new employees generally have.

3. After all modules are completed, the employee and supervisor sign off on a form that is sent to Human Resources for retention in the employee's file.

4. Supervisors also work with their new employees as they take the class. This is important to ensure that accurate learning is being transferred.

5. After three months, the employees are surveyed to check for retention and understanding of the content that is presented in the onboarding class.

Variations

• A small group of new employees may go through the class together. They should do one or two modules at a time and discuss each one after it is presented.

- There are several online classes connected to the onboarding class, such as "Understanding the Performance Review" and "How to Conduct a Performance Review." These are required classes and are best taken on an individual basis.

- Supervisors and managers may choose to use the content from the required classes as topics for their group meetings in order to clear up any misunderstandings.

Case Example

The class starts out with a video welcome from the fire chief. It proceeds with a brief organizational chart that links to each department with a description of its function. Key managers, such as the HR director, division chiefs, and finance director, are pictured. These pictures help acquaint new employees with them because they may meet them or be contacted by them in the future.

The history of the organization is presented, outlining significant changes. Since the organization is spread throughout Orange County, there is information within this class to show where all of the stations are located and those individuals who are in charge.

This class is only as good as the content. It is critical that current content be maintained so that this is a class that can never be put on a shelf. It must be continually updated, which requires considerable cooperation from all of the departments and managers.

Contributed by Linda Kulp, Organizational Training & Development.

Unique Online Situations

Virtual online trainers find themselves facilitating many kinds of events. We've included here a couple of them that may be commonplace to some people but very unique to others. In this section, you will find a process for learning about global needs of an organization, an online orientation, and a process to use for successfully facilitating a team-building session (or any other topic) as a guide from afar.

19   Corporate Global Survey

_____ Overview _____

Use this strategy to facilitate a virtual discussion to learn about global needs. A virtual discussion allows everyone around the globe to attend, and provides information and direction to the organization.

Participants

10–20 key Human Resources, talent development, communications, or other thought leaders in the organization

Procedure

1. Using a survey tool that your organization utilizes or something as simple as SurveyMonkey, send a link to all participants about three weeks in advance of your meeting.

2. Compile the results of the surveys and email them to the participants.

3. At least one week before the virtual meeting, create a discussion board where participants can download the results and respond to several questions that you have posted, such as:

   ♦ Given these results, which do you think is the most urgent?

   ♦ Given these results, which do you think is the most important?

   ♦ What is the most exciting thing about these results?

   ♦ What is the most disconcerting thing about these results?

4. Compile comments in advance of the meeting.

5. At the meeting, review the surveys and comments.

6. In a 90-minute meeting, you should be able to review the comments and come to some agreement about a general direction with ideas and a rationale.

7. Before the next meeting, gather supporting data and begin to solidify recommendations and an action plan.

Variations

- You could do much of the survey work online and then switch to an in-person meeting.

- This process can work for almost any organizational topic.

Case Example

A software company with employees on three continents was concerned about decreasing employee satisfaction scores in several areas throughout the world. The scores correlated to high turnover in the same areas. After reading the most recent employee satisfaction survey results, company leaders decided to create a global task force to review several basics. They decided to start with the talent development area. The survey they used prior to the first meeting asked the thought leaders to use a 1–5 Likert scale to rate items about how well the company was doing on things such as:

- Building awareness of cultural diversity
- Creating engaged employees
- Aligning organizational strategy with workforce planning
- Creating geographically dispersed talent with shared experiences
- Building global competency
- Creating talent that can function both globally and locally
- Filling a talent pool that ensures retaining top talent
- Disseminating business norms that prevent misunderstandings

20 Find It

_____ **Overview** _____

This is a way to assist employees in getting to know a company's intranet or Internet. It can be done virtually, synchronously, or asynchronously.

Participants

All new employees

Procedure

1. Use an icebreaker to meet the new employees virtually and take care of any announcements.

2. Give participants a list of facts about the organization that they need to find or locations that they should visit.

3. Include any passwords or access information needed.

4. Establish a time to complete the list and have them log back on to the next phase of the session at that time.

5. Review their answers and correct anything that was difficult to find.

Variations

- You may wish to put the participants into small groups to check their answers first. This also allows them to meet other new employees.

- You can use this time to check out a competitor's offerings, on a company intranet or Internet site, as a way for people to get acquainted with a new software or to acclimate to a new or redesigned SharePoint site.

- This can be done in a classroom or in a synchronous or asynchronous online class.

Case Example

Have new employees find information from the company's intranet site, such as the following:

- Who is the VP of finance?
- What is the current stock price?
- How many SKUs are in the U.S. product line?
- What product lines are for sale in Canada?
- Where do you access expense reporting?
- What is the phone number for customer service?
- In how many regions does the company have offices?
- What is the minimum order for buying foam products?
- How do you order product brochures?
- What is the process for ordering product samples?
- What is the next company holiday?

Contributed by Renie McClay, Inspired Learning, LLC.

21   Facilitating from Afar

_____ Overview _____

A strategy to keep participants engaged when they are together but you are facilitating from a remote location and cannot see them.

Participants

4–50 participants in a distant location

Procedure

1. Your success lies in the preparation. Prior to the learning event, designate a "focal" on-site person to be your "eyes and ears" on the ground. This person acts as an extension of you, providing information such as when people finish writing during an assigned activity. The focal can be one of the participants and will need to be able to focus attention on both the activities and your requests.

2. Talk with your focal presession about how the two of you will operate as a team. Let the focal know what to expect, what you will need, and when you will need it. Provide an agenda and decide how you will get the focal's attention.

3. Ask your focal or the client to send you a picture of the room setup. This enables you to visualize the room and be more natural in your facilitation, and helps you in choosing activities that will work best, given the room's configuration.

4. Utilize prework with the learners to set expectations for the session and to maximize your use of your time together.

5. Gain information about the group in advance, such as their names, roles, and expectations for the session. If you can get photos of them, that is even better.

6. Design a variety of activities to keep participants engaged, just as you would for an in-person session.

7. Use a PowerPoint slide deck to direct the participants' focus. Follow Power-Point best practice design (such as using visuals and minimizing words) for content; however, be more explicit with writing out directions for activities.

8. Insert a photo of yourself (preferably of you "in action" facilitating) on an Introduction slide following the title slide. Immediately introduce yourself as the session starts. This helps participants create a visual image of you and a more personal connection so that you are more real than just a virtual voice.

9. Wear a headset, preferably wireless, so that you can move about as you facilitate. This exudes more energy in your voice. Log in at least 30 minutes prior to the session, just as you would if you arrived at least 30 minutes prior to a face-to-face session.

10. Make a few "opening remarks" explaining how the session will transpire immediately following your introduction. This should be more than an agenda. Explain that the session will be interactive, what you will do to gain their attention after the activities, any requests you have regarding participation, and so forth. Ask for their questions and provide clarification immediately. This sets the tone for a successful, interactive session.

11. Use the participants' names throughout the session.

12. Put time allotments in your PowerPoint presentation (such as five minutes for a partner discussion) and then use your web-sharing system (such as AnyMeeting or WebEx) "annotation tools" to count down the time. Draw a line through the initial time and write in the new time at the halfway point and then at a one-minute warning.

13. When the allotted activity time has expired, use your annotation tools to write "Please Stop" in large letters across the activity slide. This will better capture both your focal's attention and the participants' attention than if you just advanced to a new slide.

14. End in time to conduct a wrapup that includes how participants will use their knowledge and skills in the workplace.

Variation

This process works for all content.

Case Example

A team-building session for a group of 25 participants located in Dubai, was facilitated virtually from a home office in St. Louis, Missouri. The session was held at 6:00 a.m. U.S. time (3:00 p.m. Dubai time). Participants completed the Everything DiSC workplace assessment as prework, including printing their reports and reading certain pages. The facilitator printed a group report so that she would have their names and communication styles in front of her. She used this information throughout the two-hour session. At the close, one participant shared that he had been skeptical about the effectiveness of the session. He said that the session exceeded his expectations because the session design, facilitation techniques, and use of the tools made it feel as if the facilitator was there with them.

Contributed by Sharon Wingron, Wings of Success LLC.

Technology Tactics

Blended Solutions

B lended learning—everything could fit in this category, but it is "how" it fits in that makes it a "blended solution." Just because you have a combination of a video, an asynchronous activity, and a classroom module does not make it "blended learning." Instead, "blended learning" means that you have chosen the best delivery methodologies to accomplish specific objectives. Organizations use blended learning to increase instructional value by searching for places where costs can be minimized and technology maximized. This does not mean looking for the "cheapest" way. It means looking for the *best* way to deliver training where and when it is needed. So, whether you call it blended learning, a flipped classroom, or something else, the key to your learners' success will be whether you have matched the right delivery mode to the right objective.

22   Move to the Goal

_____ **Overview** _____

Use this blended strategy to help learners move toward the objectives they desire.

Participants

5–30 in a learning situation

Procedure

1. Prior to the session, set up a course blog and have participants download an overview of the course content. This should be more than the agenda but not more than two to three pages of reading materials.

2. Participants should also download their prework, which is to identify two to five goals that they want to complete during the session. If the topic is conducive to a supervisor's involvement, include a couple of questions and/or discussion points to guide a discussion between the supervisor and the learners.

3. In the training room, have one wall designated as "goal post." You can simply use a sign saying "Goal Post" on the wall or you can be creative and add a drawing of a goal post.

4. Seat participants in groups of five to seven. Ask them to discuss their prework assignment and to share their learning objectives with the group.

5. Ask participants to write their most important learning objectives on a colorful sticky note. If they have more than one, ask them to use separate sticky notes for each, but ask them to keep it to a maximum of three per participant. Tell them to add their name to the sticky notes and to stick them on the first page in their notebooks. They will use them later in the session.

6. On a flipchart, consolidate the learning objectives by asking each group to identify their objectives. Avoid repeating the same objectives on the

flipchart. Tape the flipchart sheet containing the learning objectives under the "Goal Post."

7. Tell participants, "Throughout the program, it is your task to achieve your learning objectives by asking questions and sharing your knowledge and experience." Also say, "The flipchart at the Goal Post will serve as a reminder of our objectives and help us to focus."

8. Tell participants that during the discussions or at the end of sessions, whenever they feel that their questions have been satisfactorily answered, they should go to the Goal Post and post the objective (on the sticky note) that has been accomplished. The objective is to have all of the learning objectives met and all of the notes stuck to the Goal Post.

9. Whenever participants stick notes on the Goal Post, the group can celebrate by sharing the learning and applauding or cheering.

10. At the end of the session, have participants retrieve their objectives and create a note to themselves on the back of each sticky note about what they will remember for that specific objective. Encourage them to post their thoughts on the blog and to continue to share their ideas on it.

Variations

- Use colored ribbons to make the Goal Post bright and attractive.
- Use only the flipchart. At the end of each session, ask participants to stick those objectives that have been fulfilled on the flipchart.
- Skip the flipchart. Use only sticky notes.
- In some programs, learning objectives are very clear to participants, and they will identify them easily. In some others, it may not be that obvious to participants. In those cases, you may want to share brief introductory remarks before placing participants in small groups.

Case Examples

1. In a program for new frontline staff of a bank, some learning objectives were:
   - How to work on the banking software
   - How to open a deposit account

- How to open a loan account
- Knowledge of different deposit products of the bank and their features
- Knowledge of different loan products of the bank and their features

2. In a program on leadership, a few of the objectives were:

- What the leadership functions are for creating a great team
- How to ensure that change happens
- How to ensure that communication is effective
- How to ensure that meetings are effective
- How to motivate people

Contributed by Saleha Ahmad, State Bank of India.

23 Do-It-Yourself (DIY) Job Aid

Overview

This strategy takes learning out of the classroom and puts it back in the workplace in the form of a do-it-yourself (DIY) job aid.

Participants

Any number in any course

Procedure

1. Like many projects, when you do it yourself, you remember it better. This end-of-the-session job aid helps participants remember the skills and knowledge they will take back to their workplace.

2. At the end of the session, ask each participant to create a job aid. It can be a checklist, a reminder note, a list of process steps, a picture, or anything that will help them remember what they believe they need to do once they return to the job.

3. Following the session, ask participants to text the group the first time they use their job aid.

Variation

You may wish to provide colorful markers, paper, plastic sheets, self-sticking labels, stickers, or other supplies to create the job aid.

Case Example

One participant who attended a writing class created a list of the most misused and misspelled words. She claimed the job aid was worth the entire cost of the class.

24   The 411

Overview

> A learner-driven strategy intended to generate discussion in an online forum in order to generate discussion on a topic of interest.

Participants

Pre- or postwork for any participants in an academic or corporate environment

Procedure

1. Establish a discussion board and provide advance reading materials on a topic of interest.

2. Ask all participants to post a reflection on the readings that includes

   • Four key points they want to remember.

   • One example of how the material can be applied to their daily work.

   • One question directed to the rest of the group.

3. Implement strategies to make sure that everyone gets a comment on their 411. For example, assign comments or name participant leaders who will work together to ensure that everyone gets a response (usually by dividing up the participant list among themselves).

4. Provide a time line for participation (the date when initial posts are due, duration of the discussion, etc.). This is usually one week, but it can be modified.

5. Participate in the discussion.

6. If this is prework, build time into the agenda for any discussion.

Note: "The 411" is urban jargon for "information," based on the fact that many people in the United States can call "4-1-1" to get telephone directory assistance.

Variations

- Instead of having everyone in the group post a 411, name two to three people for each chapter (or article in a series). If there is a large group of people, this may help limit the volume of posts and focus the discussion. It is important to have more than one person post the initial 411, because learners will have different interpretations and highlights of the material.

- Learner groups who are active on Twitter might post 411s in a Twitter chat format instead of on a discussion board.

- To conduct the strategy in a classroom, have participants read materials in advance or consider the sum total of what they have been learning so far. They can generate 411s in small groups and report.

- The 411 is intended to generate discussion in an online forum (academic or corporate environment). The advantage of this strategy for generating discussion on a topic of interest is that the discussion is learner driven; the learners decide what is important in the readings and what they want to discuss. This can be used in an online course, in a regularly used group discussion forum, or in a series of follow-up activities for a classroom event. It can also be used in a classroom with some modifications.

Case Example

This strategy has been successful in generating discussion around a book. Each week, learners were asked to comment on specific sections or chapters, sometimes also supplemented with additional readings. Because the resultant discussion was learner generated, it was livelier than if the instructor had crafted all of the discussion prompts. It is sometimes surprising to hear what learners focus on in their readings; their key points are reflective of their experiences and worries.

Contributed by Catherine Lombardozzi, Learning 4 Learning Professionals.

25   Gear Up Your Brain

Overview

Participants review a video, magazine article, book passage, or podcast before the class as prework to get an idea of what to expect during the session and to be prepared to discuss related topics. This is beneficial for both face-to-face and online sessions.

Participants

All group participants

Procedure

1. Set up discussion areas for participants, such as the following:

    ♦ Facebook group

    ♦ G+ Circle

    ♦ Yammer group

    ♦ Intranet social area

2. Send out information to participants to review.

3. Post questions, a video, and/or a reading assignment for participants to answer (or review). Create discussion by keeping questions open-ended. Alternatively, have questions ready in order to create a debate.

4. Let participants know that the discussion comments will be reviewed during the class session in order to complete the learning objectives.

5. In the session, you may wish to ask questions such as these:

    ♦ How did this activity help prepare you for the session?

    ♦ How did the participants' comments help formulate your opinion on the topic?

    ♦ Have you found any additional resources that you may have sourced to build on this topic prior to attending the class?

Variations

- Create a video from leadership describing the class and outlining the expectations. Have participants comment on what they hope to learn from the session. This helps learners create a "buy-in" for the session.

- Post questions about the topic and have participants identify videos or resources for other participants to review prior to the class session. This allows the participants to have a hand in their own learning, thereby creating a self-discovery learning experience.

Case Examples

1. Corporate finance: Have participants review the organization's annual statement.

   - What did they discover?

   - Were there any surprises?

   - What would they like to learn more about?

2. On boarding: Use a video from the CEO, president, or another senior leadership member.

   - Have participants review the organization's mission/vision statement. What does it mean to them?

   - What questions do they have about the organization?

   - Have them go to the organization's intranet and review the benefits package and post questions.

Contributed by Shannon Tipton, Learning Rebels.

e-Learning Tools

A multitude of tools are available for your use. You are probably familiar with breakouts, chat rooms, document sharing, polling, raised hand, whiteboards, and annotation tools. But have you also thought of using a meter poll or a course map? Have you used Pinterest or Evernote or Poll Everywhere? This section presents a broad variety of tools that you can use in many situations. For each there are suggestions for how to use them. Be creative and devise your own use for each.

26 Increase Interaction Using a Whiteboard

Overview

Whiteboard activities provide a simple way in a webinar to drive participant interaction and "movement" on the screen in order to maintain the participants' attention. While some of these activities can be done using a chat box or polling functions, using a whiteboard introduces variety and creativity to your approach.

Participants

Depending on the activity, the number of participants can range from small to large. If you attempt something more complex, you should do so only with a smaller audience of 8–14 participants.

Procedures

1. Check your settings when you set up your session to ensure annotation is enabled. With some webinar providers, annotation functionality has to be turned on.

2. Prepare any images that you'll need on the whiteboard ahead of time. Depending on the activity you design, you can use a blank screen or show a visual, such as a grid or continuum.

3. Keep it simple. The "dynamic" you won't be able to control is one person typing over the top of another; however, if you use the entire screen and give the participants some instruction about where and how they should type their responses, you can avoid some of the type over.

4. Keep anticipated participant responses to one or two words, which will also help. In general, avoid asking a large audience to type in sentences, as it will get very messy, unless you limit responses or break up your screen into quadrants and direct participants where to type.

5. Give the participants a chance to practice using the whiteboard as part of a simple opening exercise at the beginning of the webinar. For example, have a

"Welcome" screen where participants type in their first names as they join the call. Another option is to create an icebreaker in which the participants type in something fun about themselves, for example, the make and model of their first car. In this way, you teach the skill of using the text tool on a whiteboard up front so that you're not derailed by this when the actual teachable moment arrives.

6. If necessary, instruct participants to choose their preferred text color when you do the practice exercise. Ensure that they choose a dark enough color for the rest of the training exercises and explain how they can change text colors during the introduction as well.

7. Once participants are familiar with the text tool and whiteboard functions, you can introduce a variety of activities. A few ideas are listed below. Use them as a starting point for other approaches that you create on your own.

Variations

- Word association: Ask participants to type in words that they think of when you bring up a certain subject. You can use a blank screen. (Optional: Have your question/instruction at the top, but leave most of the space for them to fill in. Compare and contrast the words by asking for explanations from participants.)

- Individual application: Based on choices associated with several options, ask participants to type their names in the part of the screen that indicates how they see themselves and then ask them to explain. As mentioned above, prepare a visual ahead of time and have it on the screen, rather than a blank whiteboard.

- Opinion polling: Whiteboards provide a simple, visual way to get participants' opinions regarding some type of choice. Again, prepare the visual you use ahead of time.

Case Examples

1. **Word association:** When facilitating a training session on the performance management process, start off with a word association for the word *discipline*. More than likely, you'll tend to get words that have more negative

connotations. Use that as a way to point out how we tend to stereotype this process as "bad." Then, help participants to see this word in a more positive light by explaining that the root of the word is actually *disciple* and that the focus of the discipline process is to improve the employee.

2. **Word association:** When facilitating a training session on leadership, divide your whiteboard into four quadrants. Write an A, B, C, and D at the corner of the four boxes. Ask for four volunteers. Ask the volunteers to type a short definition of "leadership" and assign each person a space (A, B, C, or D). Use these four definitions as a starting point for a discussion on leadership or another topic of your choice.

3. **Individual application:** When facilitating a training session on conflict styles, prepare a grid with each of the conflict styles you are presenting. Ask participants to enter their names in the box of the style they are *most comfortable* in, and then repeat this process for *least comfortable*. Make sure you announce ahead of time that you'll be calling on individuals for their insight based on which box their name appears in. Or, alternately, ask for a volunteer or two. This works out to be a great "team awareness" exercise as well, as members get to see where others land.

4. **Individual application:** When facilitating a training session on personal change management, bring up a reaction like fear and ask participants to type their name in the phase of change (denial, resistance, exploration, commitment) that they think that reaction will most likely be experienced. Ask for volunteers or choose a few participants to explain their thoughts. Erase and repeat the process for another reaction, like doubt, blame, energy, or creativity.

5. **Simple polling:** When facilitating a training session on documentation, develop two examples of the notes a manager would make to document an issue in an employee performance appraisal: one example reflecting the best practices you're about to teach; another one illustrating some pitfalls of poor documentation. Create a blank box next to each one. Ask participants to vote for the one that they feel is the better example by typing an "X" in the box by their choice. *Hint:* Don't make it too easy or they won't think critically.

6. **Simple polling:** When facilitating a training session on trust development within a team, create a line continuum for team trust: place passive agreement

on the left and unhealthy confrontation on the right. Ask participants to type an "X" on the continuum where they believe their team, generally speaking, is presently located. Once all "Xs" are entered, ask for volunteers to comment, as they feel comfortable. The Xs are anonymous, so comments can be directed at where the majority of the Xs landed without implicating anyone.

Contributed by Joel Lamoreaux, Deluxe Corporation.

27 Meter Poll

Overview

This strategy is designed to promote engagement in a webinar or virtual instructor-led training program (VILT) by helping learners use deductive reasoning to discuss continuums or categorical concepts that have complex characteristics.

Participants

Any participants who are learning critical thinking skills

Procedure

1. This procedure helps learners use deductive reasoning to discuss continuums or categorical concepts that have complex characteristics: for example, whether an action is ethical or not ethical, whether a comment is awkward/rude or harassing. In the exercise, learners are asked (via poll) to place a series of cases on the continuum, which is represented by a meter. These cases should not be easy calls; learners should have to think a bit to decide where the items fall.

2. The poll results draw out (via chat or open microphone) what led learners to place the items in specific areas of the continuum. The discussion can then generate the factors that led to items being pegged at each end of the continuum.

3. Set up the exercise before your webinar/VILT. Create a slide that shows a "meter" illustrating where a case example might be on the continuum. (See slide 4, the slide capture in the case example, to view what this might look like.)

4. Prepare a series of three to six cases or items that can be analyzed for placement somewhere on the meter's continuum. (You might have more if they are short.)

5. Create a poll that simply asks where the item belongs on the continuum, giving the numbers 1–9 as options. (Polls will be cleared between items, so you only need one poll.)

6. If you are using Adobe or similar VILT software, set up a new "view" that positions the meter slide at the top and the poll at the bottom. Your goal is for learners to be able to see the slide, the poll, AND the chat box all at once. (See screen capture, slide 4.)

7. Prepare to note where the case examples fall (e.g., on a notes pod in presenter view; on scrap paper in front of you).

8. When the exercise comes up in the webinar/VILT, explain the meter if necessary.

9. Switch to your polling view if you have created one.

10. Bring up a specific case, described in short sentences. If you have built your slides to do this, have key points in the case appear on the screen.

11. Open up your prepared 1–9 poll.

12. Make note of where each case is being pegged on the poll (on average, or majority rules). This can be done by your producer, if you have one. Repeat this procedure with each of the additional cases, clearing and reopening the poll in between.

13. Summarize which cases wound up on the left, right, and middle of the meter.

14. Ask debriefing questions for chat or open mike discussion:

    ◆ What led you to categorize these cases on the left/right?

    ◆ What made it difficult to decide where to place the cases?

    ◆ Some people placed X case on the opposite end, as most others; if you were one of those folks, what led you to make that decision?

15. Summarize the key points that you want to make. It is sometimes possible to have these prepared on the screen.

16. Switch back to normal mode and continue the webinar/VILT.

Variations

- Create text boxes with the essential elements/descriptors of each case example. Set up the slide so that these items appear and disappear in the order in which you will discuss them. This can be helpful online because learners are sometimes distracted and the text box reminds them what the question is. (Use slide animation tools to do this. If animation doesn't work in your webinar technology, you can create a series of slides instead.) The time you invest in setting this up may be beneficial, as it allows learners to hear the details, see the essential facts, and consider where they want to peg the case on the meter.

- A similar exercise can be run for discussions with more clear-cut categories.

- This exercise can be easily adapted for classroom use.

Case Example

The strategy has been used to discuss whether certain learning needs are best addressed by traditional training or whether they can be addressed by a "learning environment" (curated material that learners can self-provision as needed).

In this case, we have already been discussing the trend to move from traditional courses to blended learning to more informal and collaborative strategies. The meter poll explored the kinds of training projects that call for the different types of designs. I bring up eight typical design projects in this exercise. They are displayed one at a time on-screen in a short description, although when I discuss the cases, I give a bit more detail. My goal in selecting the cases was to have ones that wind up in each of the three design models, but my learners consistently surprise me in where they place the projects (they bring different assumptions to the descriptions than I do). No matter; the debriefing works well regardless.

These slides illustrate the exercise. Slide 1 is used to run the poll. The cases at the top are animated to come in one at a time. Slide 2 is blank and displayed when I run the debriefing. Slide 3 summarizes much of what generally comes out in the discussion. I reference our discussion and add points when I summarize the activity. Slide 4 is the ultimate screen capture that participants see.

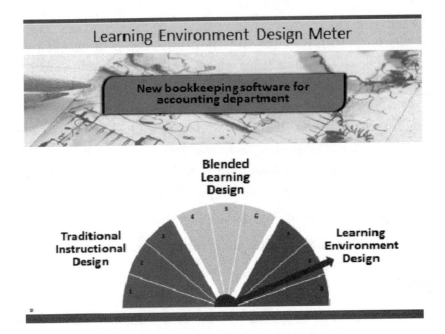

Slide 1

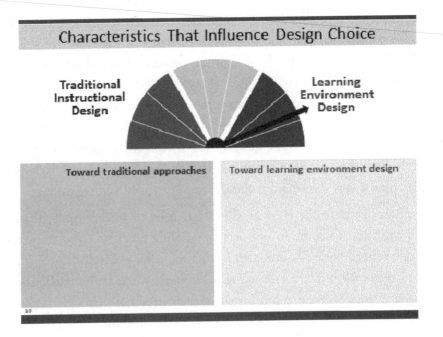

Slide 2

Characteristics That Influence Design Choice

Toward traditional approaches	Toward learning environment design
Company-set goals	Learner-set goals
Skeptical learners	Highly motivated learners
Explicit knowledge and skill	Tacit knowledge and skill
Defined body of knowledge and practices	Emerging body of knowledge and practices
Easily learned	Requires longer term development
Set in one context	Requires context flexibility
Homogenous learner needs	Diverse learner needs
High risk when practiced in work	Low risk when practiced in work

Slide 3

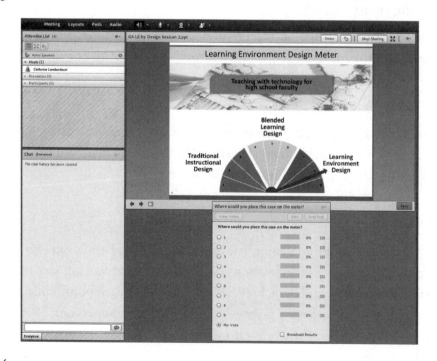

Slide 4

Contributed by Catherine Lombardozzi, Learning 4 Learning Professionals.

28   Engaging Course Map for an e-Learning Course

Overview

This presents a strategy to design an engaging and interactive course map instead of using the usual agenda.

Participants

No requirements

Procedure

1. Design a theme that brings the various topics of the content together.

2. Create scenarios that represent each content's topic.

3. Design a visually appealing landing page that gives the learner a big picture of the entire course.

4. Enable the learner to use an exploratory approach to browse through different topics rather than using a sequential approach.

Variation

Instead of scenarios, analogies from different domains can be used to grab the learners' attention and enable them to comprehend the content, for example, analogies from sports, manufacturing, travel, or nature.

Case Example

One such strategy was an e-learning course created for first-time supervisors to introduce them to their areas of responsibility. To give learners an idea of how a supervisor has to wear different hats and juggle different responsibilities, the course landing page represented a series of meetings on a supervisor's weekly calendar, as displayed here, where each meeting was mapped to one unique responsibility area.

The various supervisory responsibilities, such as team management, performance management, coaching, client relationship management, quality management, were all introduced through a series of meetings scheduled in one week on a supervisor's calendar.

The learner could click on any of the meetings on the weekly view of the Outlook calendar to begin the topic related to that particular responsibility.

Calendar

Contributed by Priyanka Malhotra, Exult Corporation, India.

29 Google Hangout Collaborations

Overview

Use Google Hangouts to have virtual teams discuss a question.

Participants

Groups of four to five individuals are ideal to allow ample discussion and sharing of ideas. You can have as many groups discussing different (or the same) topic as breakouts

Procedure

1. With your welcome materials, send instructions on how to set up a Google+ account and how to use Google Hangouts, a great job aid.

2. Class participants should already have accounts in Google+. If possible, you can share the participant list so that participants can connect with the others in advance of the session.

3. Assign participants into groups of four to five. Assign a group leader.

4. Have each group leader start a hangout for the group.

5. Give each group a specific amount of time to discuss and answer a question. One person from each group will report to the class as a whole.

6. Bring the groups back to the main classroom to discuss their findings, using questions like these to prompt a discussion:

   ♦ What did your group discuss as the key element to this question?

   ♦ What solutions did your group generate?

   ♦ What did your group agree was the key or most important item?

   ♦ What insight did you have as a result of your group's discussion?

Variations

- You can have the groups take screenshots or submit a summary of their key points to put on a class Pinterest pinboard or on Instagram. Don't forget to tell them what hashtag to use.

- Post the questions on Twitter. (Don't forget to assign a hashtag for the questions.) Number the questions. Assign individuals to discuss specific questions on Twitter. Remind them to use the question number and hashtag to make it easy to follow the discussion.

Contributed by Dr. Kella Price, SPHR, CPLP, Price Consulting Group.

30   ## Pinboard Key Learning

Overview

Create a Pinterest board for a key learning concept or for a specific class. This will allow class participants to pin resources (or even photos of their notes from class) into a folder that is searchable and can be archived for later use.

Participants

You can have as many people contribute to a pinboard as you wish, but they must each be added as a pinner to the board before they can submit their posts

Procedure

1. Send each participant instructions on how to get started and create an account in Pinterest as well as a tutorial on hashtags.

2. Add class members to a pinboard that you'd like them to use. (If you have multiple pinboards that you'd like to share, then the class members must be added to each one.)

3. Introduce the pinboards to the class at the beginning of the activity or class session. You can break up the class into groups and ask specific participants to submit posts to specific pinboards, or you can allow everyone in the class to post to all of the pinboards.

4. If you are concerned about participants not posting, you can ask them to each post a certain number of resources, for example three pins.

5. Before the close of the activity, open the pinboards and point out examples of resources posted. The participants who posted specific pins can talk about their resources. Ask them the following questions:

   • What resources did you find on (topic) that we can use to add to our knowledge?

   • Did anyone find an infographic that helps illustrate (topic)?

   • Is there an article on (topic) that we can read to get a deeper understanding of it?

Variations

- A similar activity can be created on Instagram or Twitter using a specific hashtag to catalog the content.

- You can also use another social media platform, like a Group on Facebook, a Google+ Community, or LinkedIn Group by creating a discussion thread and allowing participants to post their resources within a thread.

- At the conclusion of the activity, create a QR code to share, which links participants to the pinboard page.

- Make the pinboard secret if you don't want others to view it (only authorized pinners will be able to see the content).

- Use a planning process to collect ideas within a group.

- Rather than having general pinboards, pinboards can be used to curate specific pieces of information, such as the following:

  - Boards for just blogs that are reflective of the topic

  - Boards for just a video

  - Boards for just images or quotes

- Pinboards also can be used in face-to-face sessions as prework or in a class activity.

Case Examples

1. Leadership:

   - Gathering articles or videos published by or about specific people

   - Gathering pictures of people who have influenced the group as talking points

   - Gathering motivating quotes or blog posts

2. Customer service:

   - Examples of best practices by other companies

   - Customer service signs that reflect good customer service guidelines

   - Videos or published commercials of companies with good customer service reputations

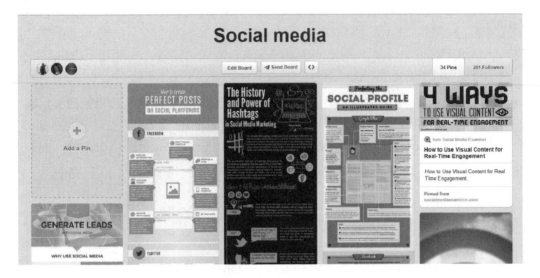

Example of a Social Media Pinboard

Contributed by Dr. Kella Price, SPHR, CPLP, Price Consulting Group, and Shannon Tipton, Learning Rebels.

31 Poll for Impact!

Overview

During a webinar, create a poll that will create a word cloud. This will emphasize a point in the learning.

Participants

Unlimited number of participants

Procedure

1. Create a Poll Everywhere account (http://www.polleverywhere.com/).

2. Create a poll.

3. Insert your Poll Everywhere question into your webinar. Be sure the question is text based, for example, "In one word, what does leadership mean to you?"

4. Ask a question at the appropriate time. A word cloud will be automatically created.

5. Create a screenshot of the poll results to send to participants at the conclusion of the session.

Variation

Poll questions are saved in your account. You can print out the word cloud and create posters or other items to enhance messaging.

Case Example

Use this tool for discussions surrounding the following topics (and more!):

- Mission statement
- Customer service
- Strategic goals
- Values statement
- Branding/marketing

Contributed by Shannon Tipton, Learning Rebels.

32   Show Me

Overview

Following the old adage, "A picture is worth 1,000 words," use this activity to increase communication and comprehension among your learners by asking them to submit images—found or created—to a shared location "in the cloud."

Participants

Nothing unique regarding participants

Procedure

1. Log in to Evernote or create a free Evernote account at www.evernote.com.

2. Create a new Evernote Notebook.

3. Make it the default Notebook.

4. Share the Evernote Notebook. (You can either share it with specific people via their email addresses or publish the Evernote Notebook as a public link.)

5. Ensure that participants have Edit permissions to the Notebook so that they can add media to it.

6. Evernote assigns a unique email address to every Evernote account, which can be used to email media into the default Notebook. Look up your Evernote account email address under "Email Notes to" in Account Settings. Send this email address to participants.

7. Invite participants to use their smartphones, tablets, or computers to email images to the Notebook, which illustrate their understanding of a specific word, phrase, or concept, for example, "leadership" or "teamwork."

8. Encourage participants to search for relevant images on the Internet or create the images, and then submit photos or screenshots of the images they created. Participants can email the media by addressing their messages to the Evernote account email address. The emails and attachments will automatically post to the default folder.

9. Encourage participants to look at the media added by others to the Notebook. Do this by emailing the shared Notebook link to participants.

10. Debriefing: Review the resulting collection of images found in the shared Notebook with the class. For example: Does the variety of images reflect a common or diverse understanding of the word, phrase, or concept? How does this affect common comprehension and application of the subject matter? How do the contributions help the group see the similarities and differences in their consensus?

Variations

- You may either download the Evernote software and install it on your computer, or you can set up and access your Evernote account through a standard Web browser (e.g., Internet Explorer, Mozilla Firefox, Safari, or others).

- Practice with something easy first; ask participants to submit an image (from an Internet search) of their favorite food. This will help them learn the process and get a feel for the technology before you give them a more complex assignment.

- In the classroom or online, you can share the contents of the folder via an LCD projector or desktop sharing tool.

- Alternatively, you could use Pinterest. Although, what works great with Evernote is that participants do not need their own accounts in order to post media to the shared Notebook.

Case Example

This activity was used with a variety of groups to improve discussion of abstract topics, such as "leadership," "teamwork," and "ethics." We all have different mental models and filters, based on our own personal experiences, of what these abstract concepts mean. Selecting an image that represents what we have in our heads provides clarity. Instead of pushing a definition from the lectern, this activity allows easy exploration (in the classroom or online) of the subject and gives us the ability to collaborate and cocreate meanings together. Participation builds buy-in.

Contributed by Trish Uhl, PMP, CPLP, Owl's Ledge LLC.

m-Learning

M-learning allows you to pair a tiny but critical (either time or importance) data point with a skill check, producing a quick connection with your learners. This accomplishes several things. It provides the learner with content, allows the learner to provide you with an update, and maintains the relationship between the trainer and the learner. Conversations continue around "bring your own device," or BYOD for short. And there is probably more concern at this point than necessary. What you as a trainer need to focus on instead is, "What does an effective learning 'module' look like on a mobile device?"

- It is concise—probably less than five minutes long.
- It is something that encourages a response from the user.
- It is something that is straightforward and easy to understand, since the user will not likely be in a distraction-free environment.
- Ideally, it should offer support or knowledge required just-in-time, like an updated policy, a job aid, or a short communication skill.

All of these activities use a mobile device—some very creatively. They do not all propose to deliver a tightly defined m-learning event.

33 Mobile Debates

Overview

By using a smartphone, WhatsApp, or similar device, this activity offers a technological approach to knowledge and idea sharing after a training session. This strategy promotes active learning outside the classroom, and it acts as a link between two separate training sessions. It is a suitable strategy to share ideas, insights, and knowledge, and it is an effective tool for team building.

Participants

Small-sized groups, in any learning situation, and, of course, everybody is welcome, from new employees to CEOs

Procedure

1. At the beginning of the training session, create a WhatsApp distribution list that includes all participants, if possible. Explain to participants the purpose of the list and make sure they agree with the rules and the terms of use.

2. At the end of the session, present one controversial question and/or problem that needs to be solved. It should be open ended enough for participants to come up with many creative ideas and solutions.

3. Prior to the mobile chatting, tell participants that you want them to express their ideas in no more than 140 characters. Point out that you expect participants to share at least one idea or insight on the subject before the next session starts. Remind them about the importance of building on others' ideas and keeping their contribution as simple as possible.

4. Close the session and encourage participants to be active participants.

5. At the beginning of the following session, present a short review using the participants' contributions to the chat. You may wish to ask a couple of questions such as:

   ◆ What did you learn?

   ◆ Do you have any new insights? If so, what are they?

- How were differences in opinion handled?

- How can you use this technique in your working environment?

6. Use the participants' ideas to introduce the next subject. This review transforms the outcomes of the collaborative chat into a tool for linking two separate training sessions.

Variations

- Twitter can be used as a tool for this type of online debate, in which early ideas act as stimuli for reflective learning.

- If the use of technology is not possible, a paper version of the activity can be applied. In this case, the activity should be performed in the classroom by adapting the brainwriting technique.

- After a first, moderate online debate, invite participants to provide their own issues. This is an excellent way to gain commitment among participants.

Case Example

In a chat session on business turnaround, the trainer starts the debate with a controversial question. After that, participants, no matter where they are, begin to share their ideas through the mobile chat.

Trainer. 18:00 p.m.
"How can we reduce personnel costs without firing employees?"
Participant #1. 18:15 p.m.
"Do not fill vacancies caused by retirements and reassignments."
Participant #2. 18:23 p.m.
"Reduce the time schedule of some employees and reduce their compensation accordingly."
Participant #3. 20:01 p.m.
"Offer to some employees a financial exit incentive—almost a layoff, but it is not."

Contributed by Teresa Torres-Coronas, SBRLab, e-Management Research Group, Spain.

34 Survey in Hand

Overview

This is a strategy for providing data on the spot in a classroom.

Participants

8–30 participants divided into at least two groups in a physical classroom

Procedure

1. Have a mobile survey tool available, such as Survey Anyplace, SurveyGizmo, or FluidSurveys. Ask small groups of participants to examine the content that you have just completed in your training session and to create a five-question quiz.

2. Ask each group to upload their quiz to your computer and assign a QR code.

3. Each of the groups should download the quizzes from the other groups onto their mobile devices. They will then take the other groups' quizzes and check them for results.

4. You may offer a prize to the group that creates the most unanswerable, but legitimate, questions.

Variations

- For a controversial topic, such as the introduction of a new procedure, ask participants to create an attitudinal survey that makes such comments on a Likert scale as, "The degree to which I believe this will solve the problem" or "The degree to which I think we are doing the right thing." Follow up with a discussion about what their responsibility is in owning their attitudes.

- You can use the tools to create a quick review to determine if learners understand the content and are ready to move on.

- Use the tools to evaluate midway through the session and again at the end of the session.

Case Example

A trainer discovered that the cost of these tools can be as low as $15 per month for limited usage. She found that participants raved about the use in the classroom and took content and excitement back to the workplace as a result of the activities she had presented.

35   Picture This

_____ **Overview** _____

A strategy that drives content home visually and, if it is located on the organization's website, demonstrates application in the real world.

Participants

3–50 from the same organization

Procedure

1. After discussing an organization's values in a class, such as in an organizational strategy class, ask participants to form small groups of three to four participants. Each group should have one person who has a mobile device that can take pictures.

2. Give the participants 20 minutes to walk through the organization. Their assignment is to take pictures of things that:

   - Demonstrate the organizational values (impromptu team solving a problem)

   - Show the opposite of the organizational values (closed door, warning signs)

3. Upon their return, have the groups upload their photos to the projector. Show the slides and have each group describe their photos and their experience. Debrief with the following questions:

   - How do these instances either demonstrate the values or not?

   - What message do they send?

   - Do you think the messages impact employees? How?

   - What would you do differently in order to have a stronger visual match to the organization's values?

   - What can you implement upon returning to the workplace?

4. Following the session, send some of the photos to participants as reminders of what they should remember.

Variation

This method could be used in a safety, team-building, or other type of class.

Case Example

One trainer compiled the two types of photos into two collages and sent them to participants after the session as a reminder of how they could live the organization's values.

36   Take My Speech Home

_____ Overview _____

> A strategy that allows participants in a training session on learning speaking skills to view their classroom work.

Participants

5–20 in groups of 4–5

Procedure

1. During a training session on learning speaking skills, encourage participants to bring their tablets or smartphones.

2. Place participants in small groups.

3. Individuals can take turns giving their presentations and speeches.

4. Choose one individual to use the speaker's phone in order to record the presentation.

5. The other members of the team use a feedback sheet that has been provided to the team for giving feedback to the presenter. See the case example for a feedback example.

6. Go around the group delivering presentations in this way, taking turns with the video process as well.

7. Encourage participants to take the recording home and share it with their children or friends for fun.

Variation

This method could also be used to record a demonstration.

Case Example

Provide candid feedback for your colleague on the following items:

Presenter's Feedback Sheet

- What you saw (gestures, movement, stance, habits, nervousness)
- What you heard (pitch, fillers, projection, pauses, pronunciation, pace)
- Content
- Eye contact
- Q&A
- Appearance (credibility, competency)
- Anything special that the presenter is trying to improve

37 Tweet a Learning Needs Assessment

_____ **Overview** _____

Use Twitter to gather data before your session.

Participants

2–200 participants

Procedure

1. Obtain participants' Twitter usernames before the training session. If you find that many participants do not have Twitter accounts, you can provide them with a tutorial prior to the session.

2. Ask questions that will help you tailor your presentation or content for a learning session.

3. Create the questions using a tool like SurveyMonkey and insert a link to the survey in Twitter or tweet each question individually. Be sure to include the session hashtag in your tweets.

4. Introduce each question with a message such as, "I will facilitate next week's training. Pls help tailor training 2ur needs with 5 questions. B sure 2include Q# w/response. #hashtag." Questions might include:

   - Q1 What is your role, and how long have you been in this position? #hashtag
   - Q2 What do you want to learn as a result of this training? #hashtag
   - Q3 What skills do you want to gain with this training? #hashtag
   - Q4 What is your biggest challenge as it relates to (topic)? #hashtag
   - Q5 How will you use the training content in your work? #hashtag

5. A side benefit is that the responses will stimulate discussion among participants before they arrive at your training session.

Variation

If you suspect that most participants will not have Twitter accounts, you can email a survey, but tweet those who do. This will create interest about the tool before and during the training session.

Case Example

The executive director of a small association was introduced to Twitter just before the association's annual business retreat (ABR). With assistance, she planned Twitter messages and encouraged attendees to do the same. The ABR always has well-known people as presenters and in attendance. A potential side benefit in this instance is that it created excitement among nonmembers, who then sought to become members after the retreat.

Based on work by Dr. Kella Price, Price Consulting Group.

| 38 | Just-in-Time Reminder |

Overview

Use a text to provide follow-up reminders or data just in time.

Participants

2–200 participants

Procedure

1. During the session, learn when participants will have an opportunity to implement what they are learning. Tell them that they should watch for a follow-up about this time.

2. Prepare your follow-up so that it is ready to send just in time. For example, if they are taking a class about how to deliver performance reviews, send the information out just prior to this time.

3. Create a learning module for participants' mobile device. Remember that the learning module should have the following characteristics:

   ◆ It should be concise—probably less than five minutes long. In one module, share a URL to content that reminds them about the five-step process. In the second module, share a two-minute video that delivers tips for having better conversations.

   ◆ It should be something that encourages a response from the reader. In this case, you could ask them if they have other tips to share with their colleagues.

   ◆ It should be something that is straightforward and easy to understand, since the user will not likely be in a distraction-free environment.

   ◆ Ideally, it should offer support or knowledge required just in time, so time the messages as close to the performance reviews as possible.

Variation

You could follow up after the implementation date to congratulate everyone. You could also ask participants to share their results with their colleagues. In the performance review class example, you could ask, "What tip can you share with all of us?" or "What do you still need to know?"

Case Example

A trainer taught a class on learning speaking skills for 12 participants who were preparing for various speaking roles in the company. Many were nervous because the speaking events were important to their career advancement. Throughout the following weeks, she would text the group short questions such as, "Have you practiced your breathing exercises today?" "Which practice techniques did you use today?" or "What organizational pattern will you use?" All participants were reminded of what they learned as they read the responses from their cohort. In addition, since she had a schedule of the participants' speaking dates, she could customize information at just the right time for each participant.

Social Learning

The advent of Web 2.0 technologies has ignited explosive growth in the use of social media tools and social networking activities. From a learning perspective, social media provides information to the people who need it, when they need it. Learners have found that the most efficient way to learn is to ask their colleagues or tap into other networking resources. Social networking allows trainers to extend learning between formal training events. Using blogs, wikis, community spaces, Google Wave, Skype, YouTube, Twitter, and other social media tools for learning will maximize an organization's investment in learning.

39   Social Learning Gone Wild Participating in a LinkedIn Group

Overview

Fosters social learning and increases learners' understanding of the importance of professional networking and a strong personal brand; requires participation in a LinkedIn group.

Participants

At least four learners are required

Procedure

1. This exercise fosters social learning and increases learners' understanding of the importance of professional networking and a strong personal brand. The activity requires participation in a LinkedIn group as a component of a course or online program. Leverage LinkedIn's strength as a mobile platform and help learners understand that LinkedIn is a great learning and professional development tool. This exercise is geared toward helping learners communicate professionally: making succinct arguments, thinking critically, and communicating respectfully with colleagues or peers.

2. Create the group, using the title of the course or program as the name of the group. Learners must have or will create a LinkedIn account.

3. Post good discussion thread questions.

4. Learners should receive feedback on the quality of their responses, as either credits toward the completion of a designated program, a grade, or badges.

5. Learners must post something and thoughtfully reply to another user's post.

6. Evaluate the success of the activity using the following questions:

   - Did the facilitator reply to posts and encourage students to reply?
   - Were participants' contributions thoughtful and timely?

- Did participants demonstrate that they read and understood each other's contributions?

- If prereading was required, did participants cite specific pages or quotes?

Variations

- Require learners to end their post with a question.

- Encourage learners to analyze and think about a statement or concept from a public forum.

- Require learners to read and comment on an article or website.

- For public versus private groups, consider a rationale for making the discussion public or by invitation only.

- Learners can rate each other's posts.

- The facilitator provides a score for each post, creating a running competition.

- Gamify: The learner with the highest score or rating wins something. Provide a leaderboard.

- Create badges: "Most Perceptive," "Most Verbose," and others.

Case Example

A course on distance education might ask learners to do the following:

- Go to www.museumofdistanceeducation.com and take a tour of the website. Provide a general critique of the museum.

- Provide an analysis of the impact of technology on the history of distance education.

- End the critique or analysis with a question.

- Read and respond thoughtfully to at least one other learner's contribution.

Contributed by Jon Aleckson, Web Courseworks.

40   Digital Round Robin

Overview

Learners engage in content review by generating and answering questions in turn. This activity was created as a Twitter-based item, but any chat tool would work.

Participants

4–15 participants

Procedure

1. Assign the learners numbers. Assign a hashtag to the chat.

2. Learner number 1 asks a question based on the course content; learner number 2 answers it.

3. Learner number 2 asks a new question. Learner number 3 answers that one, and so on. The person with the final number then writes one last question to be answered by learner number 1.

Variation

The activity could be done with any chat-based tool, such as Twitter, Yammer, Social Text, or others. Note in the case example below that if this activity happens on a very public site like Twitter, it has the advantage of providing information—in this case, awareness of issues around human trafficking—to a larger sphere of individuals than just those enrolled in a course.

Case Example

Learner 1 [@Name]. What are some less well-known reasons why victims of human trafficking don't identify themselves to law enforcement or hospital staff? #HT101

Learner 2 [@Name]. Fear of law enforcement, embarrassment, fear of retaliation on family members. #HT101

Learner 2 [@Name]. What are some strategies being used in Indonesian communities to reduce human trafficking? #HT101

Learner 3 [@Name]. Engaging girls early in money-making activities, helping young women start small businesses, implementing detailed checks of potential employers. #HT101

Learner 3 [@Name]. What are some red flags that might indicate you have encountered a victim of human trafficking? #HT101

Learner 1 [@Name]. Living with employer, employer holds travel documents, unable to speak with individual alone, answers appear scripted or rehearsed. #HT101

A brief overview of this activity appears in Bozarth, *Social Media for Trainers* (Hoboken, NJ: John Wiley & Sons, 2010).

Contributed by Jane Bozarth, author of *Social Media for Trainers* and *Better Than Bullet Points*.

41 Blog-Based Skills Inventory

Overview

Precourse blog reflection helps develop learner readiness for learning by encouraging a realistic assessment of current skills.

Participants

6–20 participants

Procedure

1. If you don't already have a course blog or other blog area to use, the setup is simple. There are a number of easy, free tools that can be used for this exercise, such as Blogger and WordPress. Sharepoint users might want to use the blogs included there.

2. Make sure the comment function is enabled and send participants a link to the blog. In a blog post, ask learners to list a few things in the comments area—up to perhaps 10—that they've accomplished and that have made them feel successful. They don't have to be work related (they could be something like building a child's treehouse or volunteering for a community project).

3. Ask learners to choose three things from this list that were most important to them and have them write a brief narrative paragraph or outline describing what they did. Have them identify skills they used to accomplish the task.

4. Encourage other learners to read one another's comments and add their thoughts on skills they feel were likely employed.

5. Offer a wrap-up of the variety of skills we use all the time, many of which we are unaware. As much as possible, offer comments related to learning and transferring new learning to real-world problems.

   ◆ Stress the value of bringing those skills to bear on new challenges.

   ◆ Note examples of the times something new had to be learned in order to accomplish a task.

- Mention the importance of reflection in assessing ourselves, taking satisfaction in accomplishments, and taking stock of what we have done and can do.

- Encourage learners to seek out and learn from others during the learning event.

Variations

- This activity was designed to be done via a blog, but any tool that allows for lengthy commenting, such as a wiki, a Facebook group or page, or a Google Doc, will work.

- The activity could be geared toward a specific content area, such as leadership, creativity, or customer service.

- After the course ends, invite learners to revisit the activity and make a comment about what skills they used during the course and how those could be applied to other areas of life.

Case Example

This is from a participant's blog comment: "From my list of 10 things, I've chosen this one to talk about. A couple of years ago, I wanted to create one of those RSA-style videos—you know, the ones with the images drawn by hand really quickly while someone is talking?—to support our local Elks Lodge fundraiser. This turned out to be a *lot* more work than I had expected. I had to draw on patience I didn't know I had. I had to learn about both video and audio, especially how to make the two sync. It was harder to find information on that than I thought, so I had to try some new ways of researching to find my answers. The project ended up requiring multiple people, so I learned a lot about project management and supporting teamwork. We had a lot of fun, though, and people thought the video was really cool."

A brief overview of this activity appears in Bozarth, *Social Media for Trainers* (Hoboken, NJ: John Wiley & Sons, 2010).

Contributed by Jane Bozarth, author of *Social Media for Trainers* and *Better Than Bullet Points*.

42   Social Media Opinion Polling

Overview

This activity focuses on using social media to conduct a quick survey concerning training design and implementing new presentation strategies and designs.

Participants

Participants include anyone who is planning a presentation or training program

Procedure

1. Introduce the activity as a methodology to get feedback from others concerning any type of training that participants may be planning in the future.

2. Explain that this concept is very simple and direct. It involves posting on any type of social media with which the participants might be most comfortable the concepts and ideas for presentation that they may be planning or designing to receive feedback from the social media audience that they have targeted.

3. Provide examples of how this technique should be implemented. The following are examples of how this concept can be utilized:

   - Say that you are planning a presentation and want to do something different than a more traditional training format, be it either classroom or a virtual session.

   - You are wondering how you can utilize different training forums, such as social media or an online program, to help present this information. You have several ideas about how this could be best accomplished, but you are not sure which would be the most effective.

   - For instance, you are wondering if you should post the training material for participants to see before the classroom experience or launch of the online program you are planning, or if you should just post an outline of the material to give the future participants a preview of what to expect. Or, you may wonder if you should give participants a preassignment exercise.

- Next, post these propositions on social media to get feedback from others about how they feel about these ideas and the probability of participation in these pretraining assignments. Evaluate their responses, which typically should be immediate or nearly so.

4. Conclude the exercise by advising participants that when you are asking for feedback, especially through such an open forum as social media, you expect to receive a variety of responses, some of which may not be helpful to the goal of this exercise. However, assure participants that they will receive honest, candid, and insightful responses from others that can be very useful and that this should be the focus of this feedback.

Variations

- Be selective regarding the social media audience you target for this feedback so as to include only those who have an interest or knowledge in training design or delivery.

- Use the same social media source to survey participants after the training has been completed in order to solicit feedback on how effective your pretraining feedback efforts were for them.

Case Example

Hi. I am developing a training program and would like to receive some feedback on several options I am considering in the design of this program.

I am thinking of asking participants to do some prereading and complete several surveys before the training is actually scheduled to begin. I am concerned that not all of the participants will actually complete these preassignments, thereby creating an imbalance in the preparation of the participants when the training actually begins. I would appreciate any ideas or past experiences of professional trainers on how to deal with this challenge. The training would be so much more meaningful if I could get all of the participants to complete this prework, which should take a minimal amount of time. Thank you in advance for your help and assistance.

Contributed by Peter R. Garber, author.

43   The #1 Thing

_____ **Overview** _____

Use this strategy to review material at the end of and/or after a training session.

Participants

Unlimited

Procedure

1. As you wrap up a training session, inform the participants of the designated Twitter hashtag (#1Thing___, for example, #1ThingLeadership).

2. Ask the attendees to log into their Twitter accounts and, in 140 characters or less, share one key point that they learned from the session by posting a tweet that includes the designated hashtag (actually, the total number of characters will be 140 minus the number of characters in the hashtag. For example, the hashtag "#1ThingLeadership" leaves 123 characters).

3. Either have the class search for the hashtag to review others' key points or, as the instructor, project your computer screen and do a Twitter search for the hashtag and display the search results—their key points.

4. Debrief the activity by asking the group which other key points resonate with them.

Variation

Do this exercise three days, one week, or two weeks after the training session to refresh the participants' memories after the training session, when they're back at work.

Case Example

In a session on leadership, use the hashtag #1ThingLeadership. Attendees may post tweets similar to the following:

- "Learned the importance of self-awareness of my own strengths/weaknesses. Not enough to know theirs. #1ThingLeadership."

- "Wow, I never thought about assigning tasks based on their strengths instead of their typical responsibilities. #1ThingLeadership."

- "Can't wait to give my team some stretch assignments to build their skills in new ways. Bet I have my own coming soon, too. #1ThingLeadership."

Contributed by Wendy Gates Corbett, MS, CPLP, Refresher Training, LLC.

44   Office Hours

Overview

This activity allows you to schedule time to meet with your learners outside of class so that you can clarify material, answer questions, and provide extra individual or small-group support.

Participants

Any number of individuals, for any topic

Procedure

1. Host "office hours" using technology platforms that offer "face time" for free, like Google Hangouts. Investing time in face-to-face sessions helps you to better communicate, build rapport, facilitate trust, and stay connected with your learners, especially those whom you support from a distance. It's an effective way of combining core formal learning with customized and personalized informal learning reinforcement.

2. Decide what days and times you are available for "office hours." Create and publish your "office hours" schedule.

3. Invite learners to schedule their individual (one-on-one), pairs, or small-group "office hours" sessions based on your available dates and times.

4. Have learners include their Gmail or Google+ information with their reservation.

5. Start a Google Hangout through your Gmail or Google+ account. If you don't have a Gmail or Google+ account, create one for free.

6. Send an invitation to participants via their Gmail or Google+ account.

7. Start the session with an opening activity that acclimates participants to the technology platform and actively transitions them into focusing on your time together.

8. Use a mix of media to see and hear your participants by engaging and inter-acting with them via webcam and a headset with a microphone.

9. Conclude the session with a strong closing wrap-up activity by clearly outlin-ing the next steps and expectations.

Variations

- Alternate technology platforms: Skype or the FaceTime app on Apple iOS devices.

- Scheduling software: Try www.tradetime.com or www.doodle.com.

- Performance support: Share a "best practices" checklist with learners before their first Google Hangout session to ensure they have the correct resources (Gmail or Google+ account, webcam, headset and microphone) set up ahead of time.

- Build on best practice: Use the Google add-ons to enhance the experience.

- Go local or go live: Use Google Hangouts to use a video and voice to meet with up to 10 participants. Use "Hangouts on Air" to live-stream the video and voice meeting and to capture the recording directly to YouTube.

- Expand your circle: Google continues to release Hangouts software for mobile platforms; watch for an app for your favorite Android or Apple device so that you can run office hours from anywhere!

Case Example

I use this process and technology platform for hosting study groups, expert inter-views, and collaborative meetings, and for delegating office hours any time I need interaction with others that offers the "next best thing to being there." You can also use this same activity to support "face time" of other informal learning mod-els, including Personal Learning Network (PLN), Community of Practice (CoP), and/or Mastermind groups.

Contributed by Trish Uhl, PMP, CPLP, Owl's Ledge LLC.

45 Quiz Challenge

Overview

This strategy uses a public discussion board and posting to review quiz challenges in an online course where multiple-choice questions form the quiz.

Participants

College students attending online courses, either synchronous or asynchronous

Procedure

1. Set up a threaded discussion board in a centrally located and accessible area of the Learning Management System (LMS) where all students from the course are able to identify it easily and return there without restrictions.

2. The instructions for quiz challenges are as follows:

   - Students post the quiz question (with a question identifier number, if available) and what answer was indicated as correct. They also indicate their answer.

   - Students include a rationale for why they think their answer should be considered correct. This may include a specific reference to the pages in the text or a citation of other course material, but not researched material from outside the course.

   - Other students who had the same question in the quiz (if the quiz questions were randomized) weigh in and agree or add additional thoughts to support the challenge.

3. The instructor reviews the comments by all students and enters into the dialog where appropriate to enhance the students' understanding and learning. The final disposition of the challenge is posted.

4. The accountability for learning remains with the students. They need to research, document, and articulate their thinking. When the challenge is in the

public domain, students stop and consider whether they have an argument, while other students learn from the discussion, and the instructor gives everyone an equal opportunity.

Variations

- This strategy may be necessary to manage time when there are a large number of students in the class.

- In a short answer test where the answer may be subjective or there may be more than one answer, this method encourages debate and could be used to reach a consensus.

- The use of discussion boards could also be used to generate questions from students that are then answered by others. Each student submits one question and others must respond to a set number. They can also disagree with other student answers.

- This may also be used in a certification or recertification process.

Case Example

The courses in the Human Resources Development online program often have multiple-choice quizzes that are randomized from a test bank that is supplied by the publisher. Occasionally, the answers are incorrectly entered into the system or the questions may be ambiguous based on the text. Students raise concerns about questions in order to improve their grade. Sometimes these concerns are expressed in the form of a hastily worded email to the instructor. Investigating and answering the quiz challenges individually is time consuming and does not support learning from the incorrect answer. Using this strategy allows students to take accountability for their own learning and potentially benefits others. Posting in the public view reduces the number of challenges when students research their own answers. The collective contributions by students are mutually beneficial and support the learning community.

Contributed by Lawrence Cozzens, PhD, SPHR, Villanova University.

Technology
in the Classroom

New tools are everywhere. Learners bring their own tools in the form of smart-phones, tablets, and laptops. Take advantage of these whenever you can. They provide multiple options for you to collect needs assessment information, survey participants, communicate messages via words or pictures or both, and follow up later. At one time, trainers asked participants to turn off their cell phones and BlackBerry devices or to put their laptops and tablets away. Today, trainers consider how they can take advantage of technology in the classroom. Activities can and should be built around the tools that participants bring to the classroom. Searching for a YouTube video or a talk on TED Talks related to the session's topic, checking the Internet to clarify a fact, or going online to find a detail in an organization's employee handbook or other document bring training to life, relates it back to the real world, and, best of all, utilizes all of the technology power in the room.

46   Twitter Engagement

Overview

Most participants in learning sessions own and bring their smartphones and tablets to learning events. Instead of prohibiting the use of the devices or worrying about participants using the devices to text, surf, or scan their Facebook page, give them activities using their devices to engage and interact throughout the learning session.

Participants

This will work best with participants who are already using Twitter; play it safe and provide a tutorial and instructions on how to set up prior to the class. In addition, it is important to review the expectations for tweeting at the beginning of class.

Procedure

1. Select and communicate a hashtag for the training session.

2. Create visuals that call attention to the hashtag and include "tweetable phrases" of 140 characters or less.

3. When you want the audience to specifically respond on Twitter, post the question on a slide with the Twitter bird and hashtag. Ask the question live and discuss it, but encourage those using Twitter to respond via tweets. Participants who are reluctant to speak up in a large group may be more likely to participate online.

4. Here are some examples of when you could incorporate Twitter to get your audience engaged in conversation live and online:

   ◆ Presession survey questions

   ◆ Icebreaker introductions

   ◆ Discussion questions

   ◆ Polls and checking understanding of questions

   ◆ Summaries of key learnings

5. Hold a debriefing at the end of the session and ask questions such as the following:

+ What key points from today's session did we capture on Twitter?

+ What elements of today's training resonated with you?

+ What elements of today's training can you implement right away when you go back to your job?

Variations

- If all participants are not already using Twitter, provide a tutorial and instructions on how to set it up prior to the class. In addition, it is important to review the expectations for tweeting at the beginning of the learning session.

- If possible, collect Twitter usernames during the registration process so that you can include them on name tags. In addition, create a list for the learning event in order to send participants targeted presession information or content.

- Having a social media team onsite during the training session can be helpful to post tweets, monitor the feed, and answer questions.

- Periodically, show the back channel during the training session. Call out key learnings and point out and answer questions.

Case Example

Twitter was used to identify various kinds of survey types that could benefit from a QR Code. The participants identified:

- Employee satisfaction survey

- Exit survey

- Customer survey for performance

Contributed by Dr. Kella Price, SPHR, CPLP, Price Consulting Group.

47 QR Code Search

Overview

Using QR codes create a scavenger hunt as a team-building exercise. This will get participants moving around and physically searching for answers. Create a theme with the questions so that participants can connect the exercise to the learning event.

Participants

A group of any size, divided into groups of no more than six individuals

Procedure

1. Use a QR code generator to create codes for each answer in the scavenger hunt.

2. Place the codes in hiding places and have each code lead to another code in a circle so that each group can start at a different location.

3. Arrange students into groups. Each group needs at least one person who has a mobile device. (*Note:* An Internet connection is not required.)

4. Ask the person with the mobile device to download a QR code reader (red laser, Quick Scan, Qrafter, or others).

5. Assign a different starting place to each group. Give each group a starting code and tell them to begin.

6. Timing is dependent on how many questions you have. Allow five minutes per question.

7. The winner is the first team to complete the activity.

8. Hold a debriefing and ask these questions:
   - What theme emerged as you were progressing through this exercise?
   - What team dynamics were at work in your team? What did your team do well?

♦ Describe how you can use the information about team dynamics to improve the upcoming learning experience.

Variations

- Example Themes Safety: Stage or find real, live safety issues to discuss in the class.

- Customer service: Find examples of items that create good experiences or present a barrier (such as a piece of broken equipment).

- Environmental: Provide examples of areas where waste or good environmental practices are occurring.

- Historical: Find items of historical significance in a corporate office.

Case Examples

1. Onboarding: Have participants find important places in their office building, such as the following:

   ♦ Fire extinguishers

   ♦ Vending machines

   ♦ Exit doors

   ♦ Director of the Human Resources office

2. Technical session: Find areas that are key to learning, such as the following:

   ♦ Equipment parts

   ♦ Safety features

   ♦ Resource areas

Contributed by Shannon Tipton, Learning Rebels; the idea was inspired by *111 Creative Ways to Use QR Codes,* by Larry Straining, CPLP.

48 Pause and Discover

_____ Overview _____

This strategy ensures that learning videos do not become passive learning experiences and that they can facilitate active learning, summary, practice, and/or application of learned skills.

Participants

Ideally, at least two people watching a learning video together; however, the video should be designed so that the concept works even if the person is alone

Procedure

1. A video is a very effective tool in the learning solution arsenal. However, a video can become a passive learning tool. After presenting a particular topic or module, have the narrator/presenter in the video instruct the participants to press the "Pause" button and answer the question or case study on the screen. Once finished, the participants should press the "Play" button to continue the video.

2. The question should be an application-based question that seeks to challenge the learners to apply what they have just learned.

3. Handouts or job aids can be referred to, in order to assist the learners with their task.

4. Once the learners have completed the task and pressed the "Play" button, the video can be authored in such a way that they must select the chosen solution/outcome (just as you would select a chapter when watching a DVD).

5. Once the learners select their chosen outcome, the video can respond to their solution with feedback, reinforcement, or even "Congratulations!" This is a very simple authoring technique that almost anyone with video editing software can perfect with a little practice.

Variation

If you have a manager or supervisor and subordinates watching together, you can give the manager or supervisor a coaching sheet that can guide the discussion during these "pause" sections in order to ensure that learning is enhanced. Understanding-seeking questions are asked to deepen learning and to enhance the relationship between the colleagues. The manager or supervisor can be guided to ask multiple questions with increasing difficulty, always ensuring that the focus is on the application of the learned content.

Case Example

If, for example, the video being presented is about how to coach a colleague who is struggling to grasp a new technical product, for example, widget B, once the technical terms of the product have been explained and the appropriate customer experience has been shown, a case study can be presented to the viewer.

"Meet customer X. She has always used widget A to manage her daily email load. This has frequently meant that her emails start accumulating and she is not able to return her customers' queries in time. How would you share the features and benefits of our widget B to ensure that she wants to purchase it?"

The narrator can ask the viewer to pause the video to answer questions, which should be shown on the screen. *On-screen instruction:* Tell the viewer to select the best approach/answer by selecting the number of the most appropriate course of action that is on the screen (this is where the simple video-authoring techniques are needed).

On-Screen Options to Select from

1. Tell customer X that you have the best solution for her and offer to send her a brochure via email.

2. Brag that you always have a four-hour turnaround time for emails because you use widget B, and offer to show her.

3. Explain how widget B has been designed to solve this exact problem, share the most relevant features to her problem, and offer to demonstrate the product for her there and then.

Which option is selected will depend on which part of the video is played to give the appropriate feedback.

Contributed by Alwyn Klein, CPLP, CPT, Learning Executive.

Learning from Many

Learning on a Team

Human beings make up organizations, create their culture, and determine the effectiveness of the organizations. This effectiveness is dependent upon how well these human beings work together as a group. Indeed, human beings do almost everything in groups. We grow up in families, learn in classes, play on teams, socialize in clubs, travel in car pools, and work in departments. Is it any wonder that teams are also a good place to learn and develop?

One of the great opportunities that individuals have for development in large organizations is the opportunity to serve on a cross-functional team. Although it may be called a "task force," "working group," "problem-solving team," "tiger team," or something else, most have several similarities. They are all created to solve an organizational problem or to implement a process that spans the breadth of the organization and requires representation from many departments—often all departments. Participants are selected for their specific set of diverse skills and knowledge.

These teams are a huge benefit to organizations, because they provide solutions to real, complex, and difficult problems. Employees improve their problem-solving skills, strategic thinking ability, and ability to work on a team.

49 I Felt Valued

Overview

A strategy to help team members remember the importance of demonstrating interest in others.

Participants

Should consist of a team

Procedure

1. During a particularly difficult team experience, perhaps following a team setback, a team member can lead this exercise to improve the team's positive climate.

2. Ask the team members to think of a time when they felt most valued by the organization and/or by an individual. Ask them to write their responses individually to the following questions on paper.

   - What was the situation?

   - What did others do to create the climate in which you felt valued?

   - What contributions did you make, and how were you recognized for these contributions?

   - How would you describe the impact the situation had on you?

3. Pause and discuss the responses. Listen to each other's situations and then discuss the following questions:

   - What contributions are our fellow team members currently making?

   - What would the team lose if everyone were not present?

   - How can we tell each other how much we appreciate their contributions?

4. Don't dwell on this activity; keep it moving. Wrap it up with quick shout-outs responding to, "What will each of you do as a result of this exercise?"

5. Ask the team members, "What did you personally learn that you can use in other experiences?"

Variation

The questions in number 3 could be tweeted after the meeting one at a time, asking everyone to respond to all three tweets.

Case Example

A team leader conducted this activity after a particularly difficult team meeting in which the group had to reach a decision by consensus. It took a great deal of energy. Instead of using paper and pencil, the team leader posted the questions on two slides. He showed the first slide with the questions in number 2, asking everyone to stand and discuss the questions in pairs for 90-second intervals. He called time and then asked them to form a different pair. He did four rounds of this (for a total of six minutes).

He showed the second slide with the questions in number 3 and used the same format: forming pairs, discussing the questions for 90 seconds, and then forming new pairs. He claimed that the noise in the room tripled and the energy came flowing back.

50   Teamwork in History

_____ **Overview** _____

This is a strategy to encourage a team to review the fine line that exists between behaviors that create a successful team and those that destroy success.

Participants

Team

Procedure

1. It can be exciting to be able to review history and learn from history's successes and failures. Diana McLain Smith, author of _Divide or Conquer_ (Portfolio, 2008), compares two partnerships.

   - First think about the Steve Jobs and John Sculley partnership. Jobs lured Sculley away from Pepsi in the 1980s, when Apple was growing fast. It seemed to be a perfect partnership until Apple's sales dropped. Within months, each was attacking the other, resenting the same qualities that they originally had valued in the other.

   - Consider a second partnership: Winston Churchill and Franklin Roosevelt during World War II. Faced with a much more devastating situation, they built an alliance that was strong enough to win a war. When things became difficult, they did not point fingers and place blame like Jobs and Sculley. Instead, they did quite the opposite. They defended each other to their critics, continued to offer help to each other, and tried to understand what the other was up against. Jon Meachum, _Newsweek_ editor, believes that there are two things that Churchill and Roosevelt honored that made their partnership work.

     ◦ They kept their mission and their relationship in mind. They knew that their relationship would have an impact on the success or failure of their mission.

- ○ They understood that complex tasks are frustrating. When they disagreed, they explored each other's views as well as the facts.

2. Meet with the team and relate the previous two brief stories. Lead a discussion that helps the team keep its mission in mind. You may wish to ask the following questions:

- ◆ Can you think of examples like these in which teams were either a disaster or a success? What made them successful or not?

- ◆ What teams in your organization are as successful as the Churchill/Roosevelt partnership?

- ◆ What role does relationship play in a successful partnership?

- ◆ What is the easiest way to remember the importance of maintaining the relationship, especially when the goals are so important?

- ◆ What can you do to ensure that you maintain the partnership relationship when you become frustrated?

3. Summarize the discussion. Ask each person to enter on their tablets or laptops one thing they will remember to do to be good team players.

Variation

A team could read an article about successful teams and glean one skill, trait, or value that leads to successful teams. Discuss this at the next meeting.

Case Example

This situation was used exactly as described to avert a LEAN Six Sigma team from becoming dysfunctional.

51   Build a Trusting Team

Overview

Strategy that explores building trust on a team.

Participants

An intact team

Procedure

1. Explain that there are four general characteristics that build and strengthen trust. Ask the team members to number the characteristics from 1 to 4, with 1 being the easiest and 4 being the most difficult.

   + Honesty and candor: "I say what I mean." "You will always know where I stand."

   + Accessibility and openness: "I'll tell you all about me." "Let's keep our agenda open and have fun."

   + Approving and accepting: "I value people and diverse perspectives." "You can count on being heard without any judgment or criticism."

   + Dependability and trustworthiness: "I do what I say I will do." "I keep my promises." "You can count on me."

2. Have team members discuss these four characteristics and share which is their easiest and which is their most difficult.

3. Explain that what each team member perceives as easiest is the strength that is natural to that person. It is the natural way that the person goes about building trust with others. The characteristics that are more difficult are important to others who do not have those same characteristics and who value those trust-building skills. Those are the ones you need to work on to improve.

4. Ask the team members, "All four of the trust-building characteristics are either strengths and admired or weaknesses and not necessarily respected by all team

members. The trust-building characteristic that is easiest for each of us, is also our strength; our weakest trust-building characteristics are those that are not easy and not admired by us. What does this mean to you?

5. What do you think this means in relationship to teams? To this team, in particular?

6. What can you do to strengthen your team, now that you have this information? List one item on your laptop or tablet that you will do as a result of this activity.

Variation

Have team members form groups based on the characteristic that was the easiest for them and discuss what that characteristic means that others need to do. Share this with the larger group. Next, form groups based on the characteristic that was the most difficult. How many repeats are there from the first small group? There often will be, because the easiest and most difficult are usually opposites for everyone.

Case Example

This activity was used to wrap up a team-building exercise following the dissemination of communication styles information. There is a direct correlation between trust characteristics and communication styles characteristics such as the DiSC.

52   Feedback for the Team

Overview

Strategy that provides feedback to the team.

Participants

A complete team

Procedure

1. Invite a facilitator from a different part of the organization to come in and observe a team meeting.

2. Ask that facilitator to provide feedback and observations to the team.

3. After they receive the feedback, ask the team what they want to do about the feedback.

4. Following the team's decision, ask each person to take responsibility for one thing that they will do better in all situations based on what they learned.

Variations

- The team could create a checklist of the kinds of things that they want their team to be doing or not. Each person would evaluate the teamwork throughout the meeting and provide feedback to teach the others after the meeting.

- Don't tell the team why the facilitator is attending the meeting if you think team members will change their behavior.

Case Example

The following are examples of what the facilitator could evaluate:

- The meeting had clear goals.
- Participation was balanced.

- Communication was open and clear.
- Everyone had an opportunity to speak up.
- The best decisions were reached efficiently.
- Conflict was managed.
- Leadership was participative.
- The atmosphere was positive.

53   MVP Award

_____ Overview _____

> This is a strategy that is designed to help learners understand what they can do to improve their team's effectiveness.

Participants

A complete team

Procedure

1. Ask the team members what it takes to be an MVP (most valuable player) in a sport (be specific if you wish). Discuss.

2. Say to the team members, "If you were to have an MVP award for this team, what behaviors would it require?" Write one behavior per index card and up to five different behaviors on five different cards. Allow about five minutes for this step.

3. Gather the cards, shuffle them, and deal them out equally to the team members.

4. Ask the team members to form a circle around a table and arrange all of the index cards in a stack, matching the behaviors that belong together.

5. Once the final groups are complete, list the key behaviors on a whiteboard or flipchart.

6. Ask the team members, "On a scale of 1–10, how would your team rate?" Would your team be a contender for an MVP award? Why or why not?

7. What can each of you do to improve your MVP standings as a team? As individuals?

Variation

In small groups, have team members find a video clip of an MVP and make notes about what they observe about that person's demeanor, behaviors, skills, teamwork, and other factors. Discuss this as a large group.

Case Example

One team made changes midstream and awarded themselves an MVP award at the end of the project during their team celebration.

My Mentor and Me

Mentoring offers a very special learning opportunity. A mentoring partnership is an agreement between two people in which they share experiences and expertise to facilitate personal and professional growth. Mentoring provides an approach for less experienced employees to learn and hone skills that will make them more effective. Usually, these skills are *not* job-related skills; rather, they are skills that help the protégé understand the organization's rationale for changes, relationships between departments, and how to overcome negative behaviors that may prevent an employee from being promoted. A mentor can help a protégé understand the factors affecting decision making, address problem solving, handle interpersonal relationships, develop leadership abilities, address technical deficiencies, and suggest new communication skills that could be developed. Mentoring can significantly improve an employee's personal interactions, which, in turn, can incrementally improve the employee's chances for a successful career.

We typically think of mentoring in the traditional format just explained, but there are other forms of mentoring.

- Virtual mentoring, when the partners are not in the same area and communicate via Skype and email.
- Reverse mentoring, when a younger employee mentors a more senior person to offer skills such as the effective use of social media or m-learning.
- Peer mentoring, when colleagues offer knowledge and guidance to each other.
- Group mentoring, when a skilled person of authority, such as an author or a guru, agrees to work with a small group aimed at a narrow skill set.
- Situational mentoring, when an individual has an immediate short-term need and may need guidance or advice from more than one person.

54 Discussion Starters

_____ Overview _____

This is a strategy that takes advantage of content that has been recently published in a newspaper, magazine, or blog as a "discussion starter" between mentors and protégés.

Participants

A mentor and a protégé

Procedure

1. While reading newspapers, journals, websites, or blogs, watch for articles that could be the basis for an interesting or thought-provoking discussion. For example, _Forbes_ ran an article on the Internet entitled, "The Most Successful Leaders Do 15 Things Automatically, Every Day." This article was filled with excellent advice. The premise of the article was that leadership is learned behavior that becomes unconscious and automatic over time. The article provided fodder for discussion that could be as in depth as a mentor or a protégé would like. A recent article by Jack Zenger and Joe Folkman for CNN, "7 Habits of highly **IN**effective people," was similar, but it took the opposite approach. You probably read at least one article every day that would be a good discussion starter.

2. If you are the coordinator for your mentoring program, email the article to all of the mentor/protégé partnerships. Accompany the article with questions that can help the team dig deeper into the article.

Sample Questions for the Protégé

- Which of the 15 behaviors do you do naturally?

- Can you give examples of how you demonstrated these behaviors yesterday?

- Which of the 15 behaviors do you wish you did regularly?

- What inhibits you from doing any of these behaviors?

- How do these behaviors fit in with your company's culture?

- What do you think you will do as a result of our conversation?

Sample Questions for the Mentor

- The list of 15 behaviors is a long list; which 5 are the most critical for you?

- How did you learn these behaviors?

- How can the protégé practice these behaviors?

- What behaviors are important but may not be on this list?

3. Follow up to discover how well the articles that you sent are hitting the mark. What behaviors would the mentor/protégé partners like to see occur more often?

Variations

- Around the first of the year—a time during which people often make personal resolutions—many publications publish articles that address the topic, such as "50 Things You Must Do in Your Lifetime." Many of these are fun to send at this time.

- You could tap into a news item or current event that affects business as the key resource.

Case Example

The article, "50 Things You Must Do in Your Lifetime," was emailed to 25 pairs of mentors and protégés at an R&D organization. Some partners said the article was so interesting that they passed it on to other colleagues in their departments and took them home to share with their spouses.

55   Take Me with You

_____ **Overview** _____

A strategy for creating opportunities for protégés to attend high-level meetings.

Participants

A mentor and a protégé

Procedure

1. Employees rarely get an opportunity to attend meetings that organizational leaders attend. With minimum planning, a mentor can provide this opportunity. Suggest to mentors that this is a good learning experience for employees.

2. Have the mentor prepare the protégé: what to wear, what to expect, where to sit, how the protégé will be introduced and to whom, and where to meet the mentor prior to the meeting.

3. Encourage the two to meet after an event like this one, since it is likely that the protégé will have questions.

Variation

Another good experience is for the protégé to shadow the mentor for a day.

Case Example

The warehouse foreman had never been to the fourteenth floor of the headquarters building, let alone in a meeting that was run by the VP of Manufacturing. His mentor took him to one, and it was a great learning experience. Even with the preparation provided by the mentor, the foreman was still not sure of everything that was going on. He took copious notes and asked lots of questions of his mentor following the meeting.

56 Mentor Meet and Greet

Overview

This strategy creates an opportunity for mentors and protégés to meet in a comfortable setting for the first time while learning more about the mentoring program in their organization and enjoying training about how to make the partnership work.

Participants

Mentor and protégé partners

Procedure

1. Plan to hold an introductory meeting for new mentor/protégé partners. Schedule the meeting to be held when there are a number of new partnerships waiting to get started or perhaps when your organization conducts a "call for new mentors and protégés."

2. Create an agenda that covers several things, such as the following:

   - Definition of a mentor's role
   - Definition of a protégé's role
   - The program's objectives and the process
   - Why the organization has a mentoring program
   - Time for the mentor/protégé pairs to get to know each other
   - Helping the pairs begin the process of completing their partnership agreement
   - Guidelines about time investment, location, and frequency of meetings
   - Suggestions for activities that the pairs could do together
   - Confidentiality

3. One activity that serves as a good icebreaker is to put all protégés in one group and all mentors in another group. Have the protégés brainstorm a list of all the things they think make a great mentor. Have the mentors brainstorm a list of all the things that make a great protégé. Have them exchange lists and lead a discussion about the lists. A case example is given.

4. Before everyone leaves, ensure that the partners schedule their next meeting.

Variation

If you have a mentor and protégé pair waiting to begin working together but a welcoming introductory meeting is a couple of months off, schedule a meeting with them, providing them with sample materials, your mentoring guide, and other information. Walk them through the expectations of the program and help them begin to complete their mentoring partnership agreement.

Case Example

What Makes a Great Mentor?	What Makes a Great Protégé?
Believes in lifelong learning	Knows when to ask for help or encouragement
Is available	Reflects on situations and relates them to self
Models high ethical standards	Capitalizes on strengths and admits to faults
Is a strategic visionary thinker	Is willing to work on weaknesses and flaws
Provides supportive feedback	Is a self-starter
Is a good listener	Is motivated to try new ideas
Communicates clearly, candidly, and accurately	Is a good listener
Is a motivator and a teacher	Values challenges and recommendations

What Makes a Great Mentor?	What Makes a Great Protégé?
Is a high performer	Solicits feedback
Is not threatened by others' success	Is a positive thinker
Reflects the organization's values and culture	Embraces change
	Meets deadlines and shows up on time

57 The Magic of Mentoring

_____ **Overview** _____

This is a strategy for demonstrating to everyone in the organization what mentoring can accomplish and for informing them about the organization's mentoring program.

Participants

Potential mentors and protégés

Procedure

1. Get the word out about the organization's mentoring program. Schedule a conference room and design an informational meeting. Plan an exciting event, keeping it to two hours or less. The agenda could include the following:

   - A panel of protégés who have benefited from the program
   - Testimonials from protégés and mentors about the benefit of having a mentor
   - Tips about how to select the right mentor
   - Logistics about how to get involved

2. Invite the workforce using whatever communication methods work best in your organization.

3. Plan to have plenty of printed information available or provide URLs where information can be downloaded.

4. If your organization has an application, provide a paper copy, even if the application needs to be completed online, so that participants understand what the application requires.

5. All attendees should leave knowing about the organization's program as well as what mentoring is and is not.

6. Ensure that before the participants leave, they know what they need to do next to get involved.

Variations

- Instead of opening this up to the entire organization, you could do something on a smaller scale and conduct it within each department.

- You could do this as a brown-bag meeting.

Case Example

An organization decided to open up the mentoring program midyear. The Talent Manager created an event to help people learn more about the organization's program. He interjected excitement and fun around the theme, "The Magic of Mentoring." He hung posters like the one on the next page, served donut holes out of plastic magicians' hats along with coffee, and invited everyone in the organization.

The Magic of Mentoring
Star in your own future. . .

Success is not "smoke and mirrors"

Get a mentor to reveal the best of you

13 May
10:00 to 11:59
Conference Room 1203
For Mentors and Protégés

☐ Learn about the Mentoring Program
☐ Tricks to selecting the right mentor
☐ No Illusion: Mentoring tips from an expert panel
☐ Be enchanted: Assist a protégé

Put a little magic in your future

Find your magic in mentoring!

Donuts
Door Prizes
Dozens of Ideas

Prediction: 2016 will be a very good year!

Sponsored by the Office of the Talent Manager

Poster for a Mentoring Program

58   Find the Perfect Mentor

Overview

This strategy provides a list of questions that can be used to find a mentor who is a good match for a protégé.

Participants

Future protégés

Procedure

1. If the organization expects protégés to identify possible mentors and interview them, provide guidance about the kind of questions protégés may want to ask.

2. The list in the case example will get you started. Make copies and share with future protégés.

Variation

You may wish to ask protégés to identify a list of reasons they want to have a mentor in order to help them narrow down what they are looking for before scheduling interviews.

Case Example

Interview Questions to Ask a Potential Mentor   How do you decide if someone is the right mentor for you? Consider an interview with focused questions. Clarify your objectives to ensure you accomplish what you need in the interview:

- Do you want to learn more about the person's job and/or profession?
- Do you want to learn something about the potential mentor?
- Do you hope a mentor will advise you about career progression, personal development, or both?

Clear objectives help you identify the right questions to ask. Be selective as you choose your questions. Five to seven calculated, open-ended questions will generally provide the basis for an informative interview. Have a couple of extra questions as a backup. Here are a few ideas.

About a Specific Profession

- Who had the most significant impact on your choice of career?
- What's the best part of your current position? The most frustrating part?
- Why did you choose to be a _____?
- If you were trying to dissuade me from becoming a _____, what would you say?
- If you were trying to convince me to become a _____, what would you say?
- What are the rewards of reaching a senior leadership position? What are the disappointments?
- If you had it to do over again, what would you do differently?
- What experiences have you had that best prepared you for your position?
- What trends or challenges do you see for people in your position in the future?
- What other opportunities exist for me in this field?
- Whom do you most admire and why?

About Leadership

- How do you identify a good leader?
- What do you think leaders of the future will need to do differently than today?
- How do leaders learn to lead?
- What is your view of your organization's purpose and direction?
- What excites you about the future of your organization?
- How important are workplace ethics to you—for a person and for the organization?

- With all that you do, how do you stay current with research, topics in your field, corporate issues, federal changes, and other things?

- What motivated you to reach your position? What continues to motivate you now?

- What is the most rewarding part of your job, and what is the least?

- If there is one thing you still want to achieve in your current position, what is it?

- What legacy do you want to leave behind?

Additional Questions

- Whom else should I talk with?

- Would you consider being my mentor? If yes, what is the next step?

- What could we each gain from a mentoring relationship?

- What preferences do you have as a mentor?

- Describe your ideal protégé.

- Who mentored you, and how did you find a mentor?

- What advice do you have for me for choosing a mentor?

- What did you think I might ask you about but did not?

59 First-Time Mentor

Overview

A strategy for putting first-time mentors at ease with understanding how to do the job.

Participants

A mentor and a protégé

Procedure

1. Mentors serve many roles to help protégés. At times they act as consultants, orchestrators, advisors, challengers, and helpers. Mentors share knowledge, insight, and wisdom. They facilitate employee growth, development, and exposure. If this is a mentor's first time, provide the following general guidelines:

   - Ask questions. This is more important than having answers.

   - Listen. To be a good mentor, listen more than you talk.

   - Tell stories. When you do give advice, you will have more impact using a story.

   - Provide feedback. Feedback is the greatest gift you can give your protégé.

2. During the first couple of meetings, start by creating a conversation. Pose questions or statements that will get things started and help you learn something about your protégé. Try these examples:

   - What are your most important values?

   - Tell me about something you've achieved of which you are proud.

   - What's your greatest challenge at work?

   - What's your greatest accomplishment at work?

   - What are your career goals, and how have you managed your career?

- What makes you uniquely "you"?
- What would you like to know about me?

Variation

Interview other mentors and ask how they got started as mentors, what experiences they provide to their protégés, and what conversations have been the most rewarding for them.

Case Example

One mentor created this list to remind her about what to do as a mentor.

Essentials of a Mentoring/Protégé Partnership

Questions to Ask

Early

What do you want to learn?

Where do you see yourself in 5 years? 10 years?

What do you like best about your current job? Least?

Mid Program

Whom do you want to meet?

Who could help you?

How can your learning be enhanced?

What are you curious about?

What politics puzzle you?

What improvements have you made since you started your mentoring experience?

What could be improved in our partnership?

At Program's End

How satisfied are you about your results?

How will you continue to learn?

Where do you go from here?

Events to Experience

Work on a project team.

Observe a customer review.

Participate in strategic planning.

Explore opportunities in the organization.

Attend a senior leadership meeting.

Put Me in Coach

According to the International Coach Federation, coaching is "an interactive process to help individuals and organizations develop more rapidly and produce more satisfying results; improving others' ability to set goals, take action, make better decisions, and make full use of their natural strengths."

Coaching has been around for a long time—perhaps from the earliest human interaction as the more experienced and skilled taught those who were less experienced how to cook, hunt, communicate, build a fire, and other techniques of survival. Current coaching has its roots in sports to some extent, beginning with Timothy Gallway's *The Inner Game of Tennis,* Random House, NY, published in 1974. One of the first and most influential models for corporate coaching is the GROW (goal, reality, options, will) model, published in *Coaching for Performance,* by Sir John Whitmore in 1992. Anthony Robbins's and Stephen Covey's books and workshops fueled the desire for personal development through coaching. Most Fortune 500 companies hire coaches, both internal and external, to support their workforce. Most organizations also expect managers to coach their employees to be better at their jobs.

60   Ask Powerful Questions

_____ **Overview** _____

This strategy guides a coach to ask powerful questions.

Participants

It is best to have one participant, but in certain circumstances, you may have more

Procedure

1. Coaches like to use the term "powerful question." This simply means that you are asking the right question. This could be the most powerful tool in your coaching toolbox because it does the following:

   - Demonstrates you are listening

   - Affords you the means to gain more information

   - Strengthens your relationship and shows you care

   - Clarifies your communication

2. A powerful question cannot be produced by a foolproof recipe, but you can consider several things. Formulate the question your learner needs to be asked by considering these elements of a powerful question:

   - Determine the purpose of the question: Is it to determine a deeper perspective? Clarify the reasons to make a change? Decide how to make better progress? Challenge the lack of progress?

   - Broaden the reach of the question to include more of the learner's surroundings, the learner's team or family, the organization, or perhaps the industry.

   - Plan for the function that the question will serve: opening the discussion, creating a breakthrough, giving the learner a push, or evoking a new response.

- ◆ Tap into the learner's style: Is it more auditory, visual, or kinesthetic?

- ◆ Begin questions with "what if" or "how" when possible. They are likely to generate more thoughtful responses.

3. Write your questions and try them out on a colleague whom you trust with confidentiality issues, if necessary.

Variations

- Practice asking powerful questions of friends and neighbors at your next social gathering. You may be viewed as the best "conversationalist" of the evening, even though your goal is to ask questions and listen to answers.

- Purchase one of those decks of "questions to ask at a party" games. Review the questions for creative discussion starters or question stems.

Case Example

An employee had difficulty getting along with a colleague in his office for nine months. He asked to be moved to another office. His manager believed that if this employee was going to be promotable, he needed to learn to work with all kinds of people. The manager is considering several questions to ask the employee in order to encourage the employee to realize this himself. The manager is in the process of determining if the employee is more auditory, visual, or kinesthetic. Depending upon his decision, he will ask the employee the following questions:

- Auditory: What opportunities do you hear knocking on your future's door?

- Visual: What is your vision for your future here? If you are moved to another office, what picture does this paint about you?

- Kinesthetic: How can you rise above this negative situation and move things around to ensure that it doesn't occur again?

61 Feedback Formula

_____ Overview _____

This coaching strategy presents an easy-to-remember formula for feedback.

Participants

Usually one person

Procedure

1. For a coach, giving feedback is critical to your learner's growth and development. You need to give both positive and constructive feedback:

    ◆ Positive feedback to reinforce correct behavior

    ◆ Constructive feedback to change behavior that needs to be improved

2. When you are giving constructive feedback, check for the learner's readiness to receive it. The most effective results occur when the learner solicits feedback, but this will not occur all the time. When you are giving feedback, focus on the behaviors that you would like the learner to do more, less, or the same.

3. Select the right time and prepare your feedback message using a formula similar to one of the following:

    ◆ "When you. . . ." (describe behavior)

    ◆ "I become. . . ." (how it affects you)

    ◆ Wait for a response.

    ◆ "What if you. . . ." (specify change and how it will make a difference)

    ◆ "What's your idea?" (listen and be prepared to consider alternatives)

Variation

Share your wisdom and the experiences that you've had that relate to the situation.

Case Example

A coach was trying to get a learner to take responsibility for supervising his team. During the past three weeks, the coach noted that every time the learner spoke about his team, he was complaining that the team members were not taking responsibility for getting the job done and that he was staying late to complete the work that had been assigned to others. The coach opened the conversation with: "When you speak about your team members, I hear you complain that they are not doing their work, and I become worried that you are not providing feedback and coaching to them."

62 Showing Appreciation

_____ Overview _____

> This coaching strategy concentrates on supervisors who do not show appreciation.

Participants

Usually, there is one person

Procedure

1. Meet with the learner whom you are coaching, whom you believe does not show appreciation to colleagues or subordinates. Your goal is to discuss this and to assign two activities that will help with your learner's development. Assign the following two activities to the learner and schedule a meeting within the week. Note that the directions are written directly to your learner.

2. Activity 1: Meet with several coworkers. Hand each of them several index cards. Ask them to write down one idea per card for what you need to change in order to be more positive, energetic, motivating, and inspiring—just one per card. While the coworkers are doing this, busy yourself with something else so that they do not feel rushed. Gather the cards, shuffle them, and deal them back to the individuals. Deal some to yourself, too. Go around the table and have each person read one. Don't disagree with the recommended improvement. Thank the person for the idea and move on to the next one. Collect the cards and deal them out again but this time just to your coworkers. Ask them each to read the suggested improvement and on the other side of the index card to provide you with some ideas for how to make the change. This time have them read their own cards. Thank them profusely for spending time with you and for their great suggestions. Sort the cards into categories that you could work on at the same time. Prioritize the stacks. Grab the top priority and get to work. Share the results with your coach at your next meeting.

3. Activity 2: On a piece of paper, draw a T-grid. At the top of one side, place a plus (+) sign; at the top of the other side, place a minus (−) sign. List all of the positive aspects of recognition under the plus sign. List all of the drawbacks of recognition under the minus sign. Share your thoughts with your coach to explore your beliefs about recognition at your scheduled meeting.

4. After a week, meet with your learner and discuss the results of the two activities, and create a "next-steps" plan.

Variation

Instead of the two activities given previously, a coach could simply have a discussion around the information listed.

The most powerful motivator for employees is personalized, instant recognition from the employees' managers. Over and over, five motivating techniques top the list. They include the following:

- Personal congratulations from a supervisor
- A personal note about good performance from a supervisor
- Promotions based on performance
- Public recognition for good performance
- Meetings to celebrate successes

Ask the individual to try at least one of these within the next week.

Case Example

A coach asked one of his subordinates several questions about providing praise, such as the following:

- How do you define *praise*?
- What standards define a "job well done"? How are you measuring them?
- What kind of praise do you prefer? What is rewarding for you?
- What kind of praise does each of your team members prefer?

- What opportunities do you have to observe praiseworthy events?
- How do you ensure that you have opportunities to praise people for doing a good job?
- On what occasions (group meetings, one-on-one meetings, walking the halls) do you praise people?
- What does praise look like to you?
- How can I best support you to be able to conduct more praise for a job well done?

At the end of the discussion, it was clear that the subordinate was unaware that he was supposed to be providing praise and appreciation to his employees. The coach took a step backward and gave him a copy of *The One Minute Manager* to read. Some people simply do not know that saying "Thank you" is a part of their job.

63   Coaching Meeting Template

_____ **Overview** _____

This strategy provides a meeting template for a coach.

Participants

A coach and a learner

Procedure

1. As a coach, you will have many one-on-one meetings with your learners. These meetings will be more successful if you have thought through what you want to accomplish and have a plan so that the meeting flows smoothly. Good preparation allows you to be a better listener. It also ensures that you can be more flexible should something unexpected be raised by the learner.

2. One method for preparing for a one-on-one meeting is to use a template that answers these questions:

   ◆ What is the objective for this meeting?

   ◆ What positive result am I expecting?

   ◆ How can I prepare for the meeting?

   ◆ How will the meeting flow?

   ◆ How should I follow up?

3. Remember to tell your learner the purpose of the meeting and how to prepare for it.

Variation

Role-play the one-on-one meeting with a colleague.

Case Example

- What is the objective for this meeting?
  - Create a plan to correct and prevent errors on contract documents.
- What positive result am I expecting?
  - Don't dwell on mistakes.
  - Create a plan to fix the mistakes and prevent them from happening in the future.
  - Create a two-way conversation.
  - Aim for a positive response from the learner.
- How can I prepare for the meeting?
  - Confirm dates, times, and the data resulting from any observations.
  - List all positive statements.
  - Focus on the solutions.
- How will the meeting flow?
  - Give feedback, including observations.
  - Ask for feedback on the observations.
  - Solicit ideas for correction.
  - Brainstorm ideas for prevention in the future.
  - Establish an action plan.
  - Ask the learner for follow-up ideas.
- How should I follow up?
  - Set action items with dates.
  - Ask the learner for ideas.

Peer-to-Peer Learning

Peer-to-peer learning provides personal and professional support between colleagues. It relies on two or more people providing each other with advice, recommendations, and emotional support. It is usually quite informal but can be set up as a structured event, like the Peer Coaching Circles. This is something that you and other learners in your organization can do regularly. The ideas in this section may provide impetus to encourage you to explore more options or may enhance what is already occurring.

64 Peer Coaching Circle

Brief Overview

Use this strategy as a follow-up, two to three weeks after a workshop, to support and help cement new behaviors.

Participants

Groups of five to seven people; multiple peer-coaching circles are created to accommodate all participants from the original workshop

Procedure

1. During the workshop, participants plan which target behaviors they will be practicing in the weeks following the workshop. Through conversation with peers and the facilitator, participants gain new insights and energy to turn behaviors they are developing into ongoing professional habits. Peer coaching circles meet several times, each time addressing new behaviors, at monthly intervals.

2. Peer coaching circles are often conducted virtually, but they can be conducted live if participants are geographically centralized.

3. Prior to forming peer coaching circles, during the workshop, provide participants with a planning template to help identify which new behaviors from the workshop they will target for immediate application. These are discussed and refined in pairs.

4. After the workshop and in advance of the peer coaching circle, inform participants who will be part of their peer coaching circle.

5. Prepare participants for peer coaching circles in two ways. First, provide guidelines regarding how to be an effective peer coach. Second, offer suggestions on how to report on their experience using the behavior.

6. During the peer coaching circle, reiterate peer coaching roles and ask for questions before the discussion begins. Be sensitive to setting up a trusting and safe atmosphere and provide ground rules regarding confidentiality.

7. The first volunteer is called upon to present. All peers will have a chance to present their situation. Peers coach each other, asking questions and providing insights. The facilitator then adds observations.

8. The cycle is repeated until time allotted has ended. Everyone may not get "coached" in a given meeting but will get a turn in an upcoming meeting. Everyone benefits from the opportunity to coach a peer and to observe others' coaching methods.

9. Wrap up the meeting by offering your specific observations of the value of the points raised during the coaching session. You may also follow up with suggested readings or articles.

Variation

Instead of assigning members to the peer coaching circles, allow participants to form their own groups based on those with whom they have connected during the workshop.

Case Example

Following a workshop on "how exceptional managers develop their staff every day," six sales and marketing directors from an international company, spread over five time zones, met virtually with the facilitator to discuss what new behaviors they had applied with their staff members.

- In advance, prepare advice, included the following:
  - This will be a deeper dive, designed to provide the person being coached with new insights to get around hurdles and/or adjust the plan for better results. This gives the person and peers a chance to engage in a developmental conversation that is based on questioning, not advice.

- As the person being coached, get ready to share a "short story" of where you are with your action learning efforts and be willing to receive insights from others. Focus on:
  - Desired outcome
  - What has been tried and has worked so far
  - Complications, questions, concerns that are making this difficult

- During the first coaching circle, one director described how he prepared a stretch assignment for a staff member, that he had articulated what he wanted the staff member to learn. He worked with that staff member throughout the assignment and afterward.

- Peers asked questions and offered observations about the director's approach to handling missteps that the staff member had encountered. They were also impressed with his approach and said they wanted to follow his lead.

- One other director volunteered his story and was "peer coached" as well.

- During the wrap-up, the peer group expressed their enthusiasm about meeting again, because they rarely had an opportunity to discuss their application of skills in this way.

- The facilitator followed up by emailing each member of the group an article that took the subject matter even deeper.

Contributed by Wendy Axelrod, Talent Savvy Manager, LLC.

65　I'll Coach You; You Coach Me

Overview

A strategy in which two peers support each other's developmental goals by using paired peer coaching.

Participants

Two peers

Procedure

1. This can be set up by a coach, a talent manager, supervisors, or informally by two people who realize that they could benefit from using someone as a sounding board to provide them with occasional advice.

2. Whatever pairing process is used, the two participants agree that they will coach each other. The pair decides how often and on what schedule they will meet for one hour, either in person or by phone.

3. The one-hour meeting is divided exactly in half. One person is assigned the first 30 minutes, and the other person is assigned the last 30 minutes. They each follow this process:

   ◆ Identify the issue.

   ◆ Identify the outcome for the meeting.

   ◆ Answer questions or provide more detail.

   ◆ Share what has been tried.

   ◆ Identify a list of options and pros and cons for each option.

   ◆ Agree on the next steps that will be taken.

4. The pairs meet as long as they are both accomplishing something.

Variations

- Peers could add value by observing each other in action between the one-hour meetings. For example, one of the peers could observe the other in the classroom and provide feedback on presentation style or managing the group.

- If the issues are complex, they could switch off meetings so that each person could have a full hour. The advantage would be additional time for understanding one individual's issue.

Case Example

Two employees attended the same Leader Development Program at the Center for Creative Leadership (CCL). They both received specific guidance about what they needed to do to improve their supervisory and management skills based on the numerous 360-degree feedback instruments that were used. They agreed to meet twice each month for a long lunch, when they would use this process to take advantage of what they had learned and to work to improve the skills on which they received feedback.

66　Peer Advisory Group

_____ Overview _____

Use this strategy to address a need for ongoing development of skills, to build a business, or to address issues.

Participants

Eight or fewer colleagues

Procedure

1. Form a group of four to eight colleagues who are at the same level in the organization but are not necessarily in the same department. The group should have a common purpose or mission, such as improving similar skills or trying to improve their departments in some way, such as becoming more innovative.

2. Decide how formal the group will be, how often it will meet and for how long, and expectations regarding attendance.

3. Identify group norms and ground rules, including how long the group will exist. Allow the group members to decide if they want a facilitator or not.

4. Draw up some communication guidelines for the group and hand them out at the first meeting.

5. Allow the group to move forward.

Variation

The facilitator responsibilities could rotate among the group's members.

Case Example

A group of six small business CEOs formed a peer-mentoring group called the Fast Five, with the goal that the members would help each other address issues, remove roadblocks, and advise on the next steps to help their small companies reach $5 million in revenues—fast. They met for a full day every quarter. The meeting started with a report on the progress made since the last meeting. After this, each person in the group presented his or her issue or concern in 10 minutes or less. The group spent the remainder of the hour providing advice and asking questions. The group facilitated itself.

Learning on the Job

Help Yourself

...or help others help themselves.... Self-directed learning appeals to all of us. Most of us prefer to learn on our own at least part of the time because it is self-paced and the flexibility allows us to learn when and where we want. Learners like to use their own style preference and structure; self-directed learning supports most of our natural learning desires. In many instances, we probably think of self-directed learning as stand-alone learning that requires no intervention and no support. Self-directed learning will be more successful if you at least consider having discussions with anyone who is in a self-directed learning mode. You might ask:

- What are you hoping to achieve? What are your goals?
- How will you know that you have what you need?
- How will you measure the skills or knowledge?
- What resources do you need? Books? Supplies?
- Who can support you in your quest for knowledge?

Yes, some of these activities could also be included in the informal learning section, and the activities in the asynchronous section could be included here. There is overlap. The key with all of these is that the learner must set time aside to do the work independently; the learner must desire the learning.

67 Every Day Counts

_____ Overview _____

This is a strategy for providing a rationale for developing oneself based on work time.

Participants

You or others you know who want to develop themselves

Procedure

1. If you are thinking about changing your career or moving up in the career that you have chosen, or if you know someone who is thinking about either one, this activity will provide data that can help make the decision.

2. Complete the following calculations:
   a. How many years do you think you will be in the workforce?
   b. Multiply that number by 365.
   c. _____ is the estimated number of days that you will be in the workforce (yes, weekends and vacations are included because you think about your job on those days, too).

3. How many days are left in your career? Is it worth continuing to do something that you do not love?

Variations

- Consider the following comments. Have they made you change your mind?
  - Your ability to succeed in the future depends on the changes you make now.
  - The skills and knowledge that got you where you are now are not likely to be the same as the skills and knowledge that you will need at the next level of responsibility.

- ♦ Effective managers and leaders are effective learners who manage successful self-directed change.

- ♦ Following a developmental plan can help you speed up your improvement; every day counts.

- Another calculation that you can use measures hours, using 40 hours per week and 50 weeks per year:

  Number of years left in the workforce x 2,000 hours per year (considers a 2-week vacation annually)

  10 years = 20,000 hours

  25 years = 50,000 hours

  This is if you only work 40 hours per week.

Case Example

A 57-year-old woman decided that she was stuck in a job in IT that she did not like and had not chosen for herself. She knew that she would probably retire sometime after her 67th birthday. When she realized that was almost 4,000 days of her life, she decided to start a plan immediately. She acquired her Project Management Professional Certification (PMP), left the unpleasant IT job, and landed a job with vibrant people in a consulting firm.

68 Your Leadership Brand

_____ **Overview** _____

This strategy helps leaders clarify their leadership brand.

Participants

You or others you know who want to develop themselves

Procedure

1. What kind of leader are you? Most leaders want to be better and strive to improve. Instead of a global statement like "I want to be a better leader," think about what you would like to be known for as a leader.

2. Read these questions, which are intended to help you focus on your leadership brand.

   - What do you want to be known for delivering as a leader?

   - What can others count on from you?

   - What is your unique difference as a leader?

3. Reflect on the questions for a day or more, making notes on your tablet or on a notepad.

4. Find an hour of quiet time when you can begin to create the "leadership brand" that you would like to have. Try writing a succinct statement of your leadership brand. Tweak it over a week's time.

5. Once your statement is about 90 percent where you want it to be, ask yourself the question, "In what ways do I need to grow to consistently deliver on my brand statement?"

6. List these items; the answers become the start of your leadership development plan.

Variation

Tell your mentor (you do have a mentor, right?) that you are identifying your leadership brand. Ask your mentor the following questions:

- How do you define your leadership brand?
- How did you come to decide that?
- What kind of leader do you see when you work with me?
- What potential do you see in me that I may not see in myself?
- What kind of leader do you think others see in me?
- What is unique about me on which I should focus my brand?
- What advice do you have for me?

Case Example

A young quality assurance supervisor worked for a clothing manufacturer. She had been uneasy and tense for a couple of years. Although she was bored some days, she didn't dislike her job. When the company offered a mentoring program, she decided to sign up for it. Her situation became crystal clear when her mentor, Frank, said, "The minute you know you can do your job, you should begin to think like your boss."

69   Set Goals for Success

Overview

A strategy to help you or someone else identify and sort out developmental goals.

Participants

You or someone you know who is interested in self-development

Procedure

1. Setting goals helps keep you focused. Planning goals can be a way to keep your eye on the future and stay focused. Much has been written about goals. Here are three ways to consider them.

   - Behavioral goals are narrowly focused on visible behaviors: "In staff meetings, I will listen to others before stating my point of view."

   - Competency goals are more broadly focused on sets of skills: "I will enhance my political savvy, which will increase my working effectiveness with other departments."

   - Outcome goals can be the biggest, broadest, and most far-reaching of all the types of goal. Outcome goals are aimed at specific actions taken to accomplish the desired achievement of the overall goal: "Within one year, I will feel ready to apply for a position at the next level by finishing my master's degree program and gaining the skills that my supervisor has identified."

2. It is less important that you know the difference between the three goals or the definition of each of the goals. It is MORE important that you set some goals and get started working on them.

3. Use the worksheet to identify goals. You will want to set three to four goals. Fewer may not be challenging enough; more can be overwhelming. Depending on the nature of your focus, your goals may be behavioral goals, competency goals, outcome goals, or a mix of them.

4. Complete the other three columns in the worksheet:

- What will motivate you (e.g., anticipation of a job I love)?

- What external consequences might occur (e.g., competing time priorities)?

- What difficulty do you anticipate (e.g., lack of support from my boss)?

5. Review your goals weekly.

Variation

There is no magic about the worksheet. Pull out any scrap of paper to write your goals. It is more important to keep the goals in front of you, to review them regularly, and to work toward achieving them.

Case Example

A 30-year-old woman sat in church with her mind wandering to the future. She had left the workforce to raise her family and recently felt as if her brain was atrophying. She started writing goals—not perfectly crafted "SMART" goals, but goals from her heart—13 of them, some of which follow:

- Finish my master's degree.
- Own my own business.
- Write a book.
- Give back to my community.
- Find work that I love.

Five years later, she had completed all of her goals and was on her way to a fulfilling life.

My Goals	Internal Motivation	External Consequences	Difficulty
Behavioral. What behaviors do I need to change? What new behaviors do I need to start doing?			
Competency. What skills and knowledge do I need to gain? What do I want to learn? What shifts in my attitude or perspective need to happen?			
Outcome. What do I ultimately want to achieve?			

70   A Wiser Me

_____ **Overview** _____

A self-directed learning strategy for individual skill development.

Participants

You or someone you know who wants to improve skills or knowledge with little or no help from others

Procedure

1. Review the most recent feedback that you received. It might have been in the form of a 360-degree feedback instrument, your most recent performance review, a discussion with your boss, or even comments from a friend or significant other.

2. List two to four behaviors, skills, competencies, bits of information, or attitudes that you think would make you a better employee or human being.

3. Now select only one to work on first. Define it clearly and narrow it down to a topic, for example,

   ◆ I need to listen more and talk less (listening or communication).

   ◆ I need to bring closure to tasks and finalize jobs (time management or procrastination).

   ◆ I need to gain critical thinking skills (critical thinking or problem solving).

   ◆ I need to close more sales (selling skills).

4. Carve out a couple of hours and go to your local library or bookstore. Find the section of books that matches your topic. Select four to six books on the topic and find a place to sit and quietly review all of them. Narrow your choice down to two to three and either check them out of your library or pay for them at the counter. Reward yourself with a hot tea or coffee on your way home.

5. Read the books—yes, all of them—and create a plan for how you will become a "wiser you" based on what you learn during your reading.

Variations

- Google the topic to find books on the topic and download them to your tablet or purchase them online.
- Locate TED Talks or YouTube videos about your chosen topic and watch them.
- Select a blog about your topic and read it regularly.

Case Example

A manager was told by his boss that he needed to focus more on strategy than on day-to-day work. He purchased a couple of books, registered for a MOOC (massive open online course) offered by Wharton, and created a lesson plan for himself.

71   Volunteer for a Special Assignment

_____ Overview _____

A strategy that uses a special project to gain skills and feedback.

Participants

You or someone you've encouraged

Procedure

1. Tell your supervisor that you would like to take on a special assignment for which your supervisor feels you are qualified, for example, something that requires coordination among several departments. State that you hope that the assignment will also be a stretch for you.

2. During the assignment, keep a list of all of the skills required for the assignment. Rate yourself on each of the skills. Be candid and explain why you rated yourself as you did: What do you do well? What do you need to improve?

3. Midway through the project, and again at the end of the project, review what happened with your supervisor. Ask your supervisor to provide feedback to you about your skills. How does your supervisor's assessment compare to yours?

4. For those skills where there is a gap between your assessment and your supervisor's assessment, try to reconcile the differences. For those skills where you both agree that improvement is required, identify learning experiences in which you can participate to gain new skills and knowledge.

Variation

Identify a personal challenge that you've always wanted to accomplish, for example, running a half-marathon, learning to tango, or learning to cook gourmet meals. Plot a time line to accomplish your challenge. During your challenge, track your thoughts and feelings along the way. Determine what works for you and what doesn't. How are you motivated? What gets in your way of progress? How do you manage your time? Is it better to do this with a partner or alone? At the end of the time line, did you meet your challenge? What did you learn about yourself? What did you learn about your performance? What does this tell you about how you learn? About your ability to assess yourself? How can you put what you learned into practice at work?

Case Example

A shy account executive knew that in her next role, she would be required to give presentations to customers and other companies. She wanted to improve her speaking skills. She joined a local Toastmasters International group and attended meetings every week. She also volunteered as the program chair for her local professional association because she knew that she would have to introduce the guest speaker at every meeting.

72 Notable Quotables

Overview

A strategy to inspire you or others or to provide reinforcement to others.

Participants

One or many

Procedure

1. Start compiling a notebook of quotes that inspire you.

2. They may be quotes you jot down from an article or book you read; they may be words spoken by someone on the radio; they may be quotes from some of your favorite heroes and speakers, such as Abraham Lincoln or Martin Luther King; they may come from actors or actresses; they may come from cartoons that you rip out of the Sunday comic section; they may be something your grandmother always said to you; they may be ads with catchphrases; or they may be phrases that you say.

3. Whatever they are and wherever they come from, begin compiling your quotes today. Continue to add to them in your notebook. Review them. Reread them. If they inspired you once, they will inspire you again. And if they inspire you, they will inspire someone else.

Variation

Add a new quote to the end of every email that you send. Many people add a quote—the same quote—as a part of their signature to their emails. Be bold. Be special. Inspire others as you are being inspired by your quotes. Share a different quote, perhaps even one that fits the occasion best, in your email.

Case Example

A supervisor was just starting her job. She would add a quote to the bottom of her notes to employees or to comments about their work. One day a colleague told her that it seemed like extra work that she did not have time for and that it also seemed too feminine, and if she wanted to climb the corporate ladder, she needed to stop being so "girly." The supervisor stopped adding her special quotes. About six weeks later, she was having a meeting with a staff member. At the end of the meeting, the staff member asked the supervisor, "Are you getting a new job?" The supervisor answered, "No." The staff member asked, "Are you ill?" Again, the supervisor answered, "No." The staff member asked, "Are you upset with us?" And, again, the supervisor answered, "No!! Why are you asking?" The staff member replied, "You stopped adding quotes to your notes to us, and we thought something was wrong." Sometimes it's the small things you do that make a difference.

73   Goals for Life

Overview

A strategy to encourage learners to focus on the entire self-development process in order to lead a more balanced life.

Participants

One person who is interested in developing more than just professional skills

Procedure

1. Becoming a lifelong learner is important. Creating a professional individual development plan (IDP) is something that most people have experienced. Your organization most likely expects everyone to create an IDP. An IDP helps learners stay focused on their professional development.

2. This activity challenges learners to stretch themselves a bit. To become a lifelong learner requires that learners move beyond what they learn as professionals and, instead, consider their whole life. A holistic plan includes all parts of a learner's life, such as:

   - Professional: Job satisfaction, work, career path, education
   - Personal: Relationship skills, friends, current or future life partner
   - Financial: Savings, investments, home, retirement plan
   - Health: Exercise, diet, vitamins
   - Social: Sports, activities, clubs
   - Family: Children, parents, relatives
   - Pleasure: Vacations, hobbies, leisure time activities, pleasure reading, travel
   - Creative: Self-space, spiritual, artistic, community, sharing with others

3. A template is located in the case example. Use this as a model. Learners may wish to add or delete categories. The ultimate goal, however, is to incorporate all aspects of the learner's life.

4. Learners identify goals that they wish to reach in each of the categories. For example, if they have a desire to "get in shape," they may wish to create a goal, such as "By January 31, I will go for a 30-minute walk three times each week."

5. Learners identify resources that they can utilize when they need support to achieve their goals, such as time or other people's support.

6. Learners establish goals that are comfortable for a one-, three-, five-, or ten-year plan. The key is to get them thinking about more than just professional development.

Variations

• Learners can draw a circle and divide it into eight equal pie shapes. They can label each piece of the pie and fill in what is important in each one. They can also think about how balanced their "life pie" is—that is, what percent is spent on each piece of the pie and whether that is what they want.

• Learners may wish to rate their satisfaction with each category on a scale of 1–7. Then they can develop goals for the two or three categories that they rated as the lowest.

Case Example

Holistic Development Plan Example

Category	Goal	Resources	Date
Professional	Earn credit toward a degree		
	Find a mentor		
Personal	Go to dinner with friends weekly		
	Take a listening skills class		
Financial	Eliminate debt		
	Set up an investment program		
Health	Get an annual checkup		
	Eat nutritional food		
Social	Take tennis lessons		
	Join a card-playing club		
Family	Spend more time with my children		
	Visit my grandmother weekly		
Pleasure	Plan a trip		
	Buy season tickets to baseball games		
Creative	Sign up for yoga classes		
	Volunteer at the homeless shelter		

74 Test Yourself

_____ **Overview** _____

A starting point for individuals who are just beginning to explore self-development.

Participants

Individual who is looking for insight or a place to start with self-development

Procedure

1. Do you want to test yourself—on almost anything? Queendom is the land of tests, a fun-filled and very interesting website where anyone can take a test that will reveal some serious and some not so serious aspects of who you are.

2. Check out www.queendom.com for all sorts of tests: Some you can take just for fun, but most will provide you with some insight about yourself regarding your communication, personality, relationships, attitude, risk taking, management style, and others.

3. Share the website with your learner. Inform the learner that you can assist with any developmental needs that may occur as a result of the visit to Queendom.

Variation

Pick a test—any test. Once the learner has completed one of the tests, have the learner share the results with a colleague and ask for additional feedback.

Case Example

A department used the Queendom site prior to a team-building session. Each member went online and completed a "test" of choice. They brought the results to the team-building session, and it was used as an opening activity.

Informal Learning

Informal learning is the unofficial, impromptu, unscheduled way most people learn to do their jobs and almost everything in life. Some people estimate that informal learning is responsible for 70 to 80 percent of all learning that occurs on the job. That's logical because when we are at work, we spend at least 70 to 80 percent of our time doing our job and we are learning most of the time. Sometimes it's a very simple thing, like learning how to use a new function key on your laptop from the person who sits next to you. Sometimes it's by accident, like when you overhear a discussion in the hallway about a new project on a different floor. Sometimes you find a template on the company's intranet that makes your job easier—and you may share it with a colleague. None of these can be planned; it's informal learning. However, even though they cannot be "planned," we can be thoughtful about what we make available so that informal learning is easier and more reliable, captures knowledge from everyone throughout the organization, is correct and sufficient, and uses best practices. We do need to find ways to "formally" design and deliver "informal" learning. And, most important, we need to create an organizational culture that recognizes and supports informal learning.

75 First Things First

Overview

This is a strategy that uses a follow-up tool for prioritizing work as an example of how learning is supported following a training session.

Participants

Any number

Procedure

1. First Things First is one of Stephen Covey's Seven Habits. It describes a framework for prioritizing work. Sometimes more urgent, immediate things get addressed at the expense of tasks that are not urgent (timewise) but are, in fact, very important.

2. This informal technique presents a tool based on a Stephen Covey workshop. Numerous tools can be made available to participants on their laptops so that they can review them or pull them out when they need them.

3. For this particular tool, participants can consider some of the tasks that they have to do. They assess them based on the criterion of whether they are "important" or "urgent."

4. Back at the workplace, participants sort their tasks into the appropriate quadrants. They can discuss them with their supervisor, mentor, colleagues, or others, asking questions, such as:

   ♦ What do your results tell you about how you are using your time?

   ♦ In which quadrant do you spend most of your time?

   ♦ In which quadrant do you want to spend more of your time?

Variation

Providing tools following a workshop, recommending a book, and sharing related techniques or other kinds of learning ensures that the support is available for employees when they need it to continue to learn on the job.

Case Example

Prioritizing Work Tool

Important	Quadrant I	Quadrant II
	(Crises, Problems, Deadlines)	(Planning, Prevention, New Ideas)
Not Important	Quadrant III	Quadrant IV
	(Interruptions, some meetings)	(Trivia, busy work, junk mail)
	Urgent	Not Urgent

76   A Virtual Book Club

_____ Overview _____

This method is a way people can learn key concepts together, improve team dynamics, and begin an organization's culture initiative.

Participants

Anyone who is interested in learning by reading and reviewing in a group setting

Procedure

1. Choose a book on a relevant business-related topic, such as leadership or teamwork, or something a team needs to learn.

2. Assign the book as prereading and create a discussion forum for people to discuss it. The book can be discussed in a webinar or a conference call format.

3. Create a schedule for conference calls or webinars and assign responsibilities.

4. Create a discussion guide with questions for readers to review.

Case Example

Discussion Guide

- Give the book's title.
- Give the author's name.
- Describe the purpose of the book club and any expectations for the group.
- Describe any background information that may contribute to the discussion or context of the book chosen. (Why this book? Why now?)
- Include reflection questions to consider before beginning or after finishing the book.
- List key questions for discussion. Provide space for thoughts about the book.
- Create questions to help draw out how the content applies to the job.

Contributed by Renie McClay, Inspired Learning, LLC.

77 Brown Bags and Books

_____ Overview _____

> This strategy allows a group of individuals in a book club to explore a business-related topic through reading.

Participants

3–30 interested employees

Procedure

1. As a group, identify a topic that you will explore over a designated time period, such as three months. It should be enough time so that the group can read several books by various authors in order to get different perspectives on the topic.

2. Once a topic has been determined, ask a group of volunteers to recommend several books that can be read during the designated time period.

3. Have the group meet weekly during lunchtime. Assign a book to be read over a two-week period. This means that the group might discuss the first half at a meeting and then the last half of the book at the next meeting.

4. Create a discussion guide that might include questions, such as the following:

   • How does this book support our organization's culture?

   • What is different from our culture?

   • How can we use some of the concepts in this book to improve our organization?

5. The role for taking care of logistics (scheduling a location, identifying books, creating discussion questions) should probably rotate so that one person doesn't feel "stuck" with the work.

Variations

- Half of the group could read one book and another half could read a different book. The group could compare and contrast the two books.
- Different individuals could read different chapters and report on their chapters.

Case Example

A furniture company was purchased by a foreign conglomerate. Employees wanted to learn more about what to expect. They started reading books about the company and the country in which it was based. They supplemented their reading by reading articles in magazines, news outlets, and online, and soon after, they invited employees from another company that also had the experience of being purchased by an offshore conglomerate to discuss their experience.

78   "Bugs Me" List

Overview

A strategy to improve the work environment.

Participants

Any number of employees who want to create a better working environment

Procedure

1. Sometimes there are a few things that, if they were improved upon, would make a lot of people happier. This activity is for them.

2. Start by setting parameters: The items are supportive in nature and will not change the way we get the job done. In addition, they can only affect our department, for example, we run out of paper at the copying machine, emails are not answered in our department in a timely manner, or the refrigerator in the break room is messy.

3. Bring a group of people together. Have the members of the group brainstorm a list of everything that "bugs them" on the job. Ask them to identify possible ways in which the number of items on the list can be reduced.

4. Ask for volunteers to determine the root cause of each problem and to resolve it.

5. Finally, identify a team to resolve what "bugs" them.

Variation

Start a list on a discussion board. Keep things moving by asking for problems first and then possible solutions, and, finally, volunteers to resolve the problems.

Case Example

A manager in the creative department of an advertising agency posted a note on his door that read, "If it bugs you, let me know." The paper on which the note was written had a place to list any responses and requested that the individuals sign their names. He brought the list of 17 items to a staff meeting and asked if there were volunteers to address some of the items on the list. There were several takers. He identified that the rest of the list required teams to delve deeper into the problems before solving them. He asked who in the room needed to practice leadership, teamwork, creative problem solving, or communication skills. When almost all hands went up, he said, "Great. All of these items require the same skills to be successful. Which problem would you like to solve?"

79   Give 'em a "10"

Overview

A strategy to encourage individuals to think more positively.

Participants

Individuals who have been told that they are too negative

Procedure

1. Plant this idea with a team or individuals who seem to look for the worst in others—individuals, departments, or situations.

2. Use John Maxwell's concept (from *The 21 Indispensable Qualities of a Leader*) and in your mind put a "10" on everyone and everything.

3. Individuals start by expecting the best of others and projects: Expect that the person from another department has only your best interests in mind. Expect that the new project will run smoothly and not have any glitches.

4. Is there a danger in "Pollyanna thinking" and a chance that this will cause learners to miss something or not be prepared? Maybe, but probably not. Planning will still go on. It's the best way to do business: Expect the best but plan for the worst.

5. Negativity can be contagious—but so can positivity.

6. Whether you are a talent developer, a supervisor, a coach, or a team facilitator, plant this idea with one or more people. Model it yourself. It doesn't need any formal learning at all—just practice and modeling.

Variation

Practice this at a social event: In your mind put a "10" on the head of everyone whom you meet. Expect that they will be the most interesting person you meet all night. Learn and use their names. Be positive. Be curious. Focus on their interests.

Finally, be sure to treat them as a "10." You will be known as the best person at the event—not that this is your goal. Your goal is to practice making everyone feel like the most important person at the social event.

Case Example

A university instructor went to lunch with her best friend. At the end of the meal, the friend said to the instructor, "I am not sure what is going on, but you have lost your positive outlook. You are down on everyone and everything at the university." The instructor took the advice to heart and realized that she had become very negative in both her professional life and her personal life. After recognizing and changing her attitude, she realized how much more fun it was to anticipate the best in every situation.

80   What Got You Here

Overview

A strategy to help individuals or a team to explore leadership flaws, such as those identified by Marshall Goldsmith.

Participants

Individuals, pairs, or a team of leaders or potential leaders

Procedure

1. Marshall Goldsmith has written a practical book, *What Got You Here Won't Get You There* (Hyperion, 2007), about what stands in the way of a leader's future achievements. He identifies 20 transactional flaws, which are listed in the case example.

2. Get together with a coworker and review the 20 transactional flaws. If you want more information, the book is a fast read, down to earth, and practical. Place the flaws in the order in which they are most problematic for you, from 1 to 20. You should each make your own ordered list with the flaws that are the most problematic for each of you. (It's okay for some flaws to be tied.)

3. Share your list with each other and discuss each list.

4. At a second meeting, each of you should suggest ways in which you could both improve—especially for those flaws that you rated as the most problematic.

Variations

- This could be done with your team rather than as a pair.
- Each of the 20 flaws could be written, one per card, on 20 index cards. Have your team gather around a table and order the cards. Encourage discussion.
- Each of the 20 flaws could be written, one per note, on 20 sticky notes. Put the notes on a wall and have your team gather around and order the sticky notes in complete silence—with no discussion. After 15 minutes, have a discussion.
- A supervisor could try this activity at the beginning of a departmental meeting.

Case Example

Here is Marshall Goldsmith's list of flaws:

- The need to win at all costs
- Adding your two cents' worth in every discussion
- The need to rate others and impose your own standards on them
- Making sarcastic, destructive comments
- Overusing negative qualifiers, for example, "yes, but," "but," or "however," which imply, "You're wrong"
- The need to show you are smarter
- Speaking when angry
- The need to share your negative thoughts
- Withholding information
- Failing to give proper recognition
- Claiming credit that you don't deserve
- Making excuses
- Clinging to the past
- Playing favorites
- Refusing to express regret
- Not listening
- Failing to express gratitude
- Punishing the messenger
- "Passing the buck" and blaming everyone else
- The excessive need to be "me"; exalting your faults as virtues simply because that's who you are

81   Plan for Informal Learning

_____ **Overview** _____

A strategy to create a workplace that is conducive to informal learning.

Participants

Anyone and everyone

Procedure

1. Organizations understand the great value and broad use of informal learning, but few organizations invest the time to create a plan for how to establish a process to ensure ease and efficiency of use. This strategy encourages talent managers, trainers, designers, and others in the learning and development field to create an atmosphere in an organization that is conducive to informal learning. These bulleted items are just a start for you to begin thinking about your organization.

2. An atmosphere in an organization that is conducive to informal learning starts with the organization's culture:

   ◆ Create a culture conducive to lifelong learning.

   ◆ Support volunteer work in the community.

   ◆ Value and fund membership in associations.

   ◆ Include the IDP (individual development plan) process in performance expectations.

   ◆ Encourage learning relationships, such as mentoring, coaching, and partnering.

   ◆ Create a culture that is vibrant, with daily reminders that learning is all around us.

3. Support learning for employees:

   ◆ Encourage learning on the job.

   ◆ Teach learners how to learn.

- Provide time for learning away from the job.
- Invest in blogs, networks, and locations of central knowledge.
- Make it okay to learn together at all times.

4. Keep the conversation going in your organization.

Variations

- Read *Informal Learning* by Jay Cross to discover other ideas.
- Create your own list and meet with your senior leaders to advance your thoughts to the C-Suite.

Case Example

An organization created a gathering spot for its employees called "The Cove" (reminiscent of the organization's nautical beginnings), where employees could gather, purchase coffee on the honor system, and talk. It was fitted with comfortable chairs, small tables, and plenty of paper, flipcharts, markers, and crayons for serious doodling or business strategizing.

Learn from Experience

Experiential learning provides a new way of thinking about an old way of teaching. Hands-on learning is anything but new, as laboratories have been an essential component of many educational philosophies. Historically, hands-on learning has been essential to train task- or skill-heavy jobs. Consider what experiences you can provide to all learners. How can we, as learning and development professionals, truly facilitate the learning process in a learner-centric way? Break loose from the typical learning methods and embrace experiential learning in the classroom, on the job, and in blended options.

Designing experiential learning activities in classroom activities ensures that learners have an opportunity to practice their skills. Designing activities that relate to the learners' immediate needs ensures that the skills they are practicing are directly related to the challenges they face. Bringing the real world into the classroom benefits learners and the organization by giving learners the skills required to solve today's problems and prevent those of the future. Finding ways to take the entire learning experience outside the organization is even better, and if they both serve a purpose, use a blended experiential learning approach.

As Macolm Knowles has said:

We will learn no matter what! Learning is as natural as rest or play. With or without books, inspiring trainers, or classrooms, we will manage to learn. Educators can, however, make a difference in what people learn and how well they learn it. If we know why we are learning and if the reason fits our needs as we perceive them, we will learn quickly and deeply.

82   Experiential Learning in the Classroom

_____ **Overview** _____

A strategy that presents five steps for creating experiential learning in both virtual and physical classroom settings.

Participants

Any number of individuals in any activity for any topic

Procedure

1. Experiential learning occurs when a learner participates in an activity, reviews the activity, identifies useful knowledge or skills that were gained from the activity, and transfers the results to the workplace. An American baseball player, Vernon Sanders Law, stated, "Experience is a hard teacher because she gives the test first, the lesson after." This is the learning process we go through in our day-to-day lives, and we call this "life experience." Experiential learning activities attempt to duplicate life experiences. Participants "experience" what they are to learn before they discuss it.

2. Experiential learning activities (ELAs) are based on several characteristics:

   • They are directed toward a specific learning goal.

   • They are structured, that is, they have specific steps and a process that must be followed to ensure results.

   • There is a high degree of participant involvement.

   • They generate data and information for participant analysis.

   • They require processing or debriefing for maximum learning.

3. The five steps in the Pfeiffer and Jones experiential learning cycle explain what must occur during an activity to ensure that maximum learning occurs. The five steps are experiencing, publishing, processing, generalizing, and applying.

4. You may use this process for any experiential learning activity.

1. Experiencing: Do something.

This is the step that is associated with the "game" or the experience. Participants are involved in completing a defined task. If the process ends here, all learning is left to chance and the trainer has not completed the process.

2. Publishing: Share observations.

The second step of the cycle gives learners a chance to share what they saw, how they felt, and what they experienced. The trainer can facilitate this in several ways: by recording data in the large group, having participants share or interview in subgroups, or leading a variation of a round-robin. Some questions that the trainer can ask include:

What happened? What did you observe?
What occurred during the activity?
How did you feel about what occurred?

The trainer typically begins with a broad question and then focuses on more specific questions. The trainer may probe for turning points or decisions that affected the outcome. This stage is important because it allows participants to vent or express strong emotions and it allows the facilitator to gather data.

3. Processing: Interpret the dynamics or concepts.

This step gives participants a chance to discuss the patterns and dynamics they observed during the activity. Observers may be used to discuss this step. Some questions that the trainer may ask include:

Why do you think this may have occurred?
What did you learn about yourself?
What did you learn?
What theories or principles might be true based on your experience?

The facilitator again begins with a broad question and then focuses on more specific questions. This stage allows participants to test various hypotheses, preparing them to apply what they have learned. This stage gives the trainer a way to observe how much participants have learned from the experience.

4. Generalizing: Connect to real life.

The key question in this step is, "So what?" Participants are led to focus their awareness on situations that are similar to what they have experienced. This step makes the activity practical. Some questions the trainer may ask include:

How does this relate to. . . .?
What did you learn about yourself?
What does this suggest to you about. . . .?
How does this experience help you understand. . . .?
What if. . . .?

This stage ensures that the participants grasp the lesson/learning that was intended. The "What if. . . .?" question becomes a bridge to the last step, which is applying what has been learned.

5. Applying: Plan effective change.

The last step presents the reason the activity was conducted: "Now what. . . .?" The facilitator helps participants apply generalizations to actual situations in which they are involved. The participants may establish goals, commit to change, make promises, identify how something will change at the workplace, or identify any other actions that may result from the experience. The questions that can be asked are:

What will you do differently as a result of this experience?
How will you transfer what you have learned to the workplace?
How and when will you apply what you have learned?
How might this help you in the future?
What's next?

Variation

Always create the questions that are most appropriate for your activity and what learners need.

Case Example

The "Graham Cracker Challenge" is an ELA for exploring risk. These abbreviated instructions give you an overview of the ELA process.

1. Experiencing: Tell participants to dunk a graham cracker in milk. Tell them the goal is to keep their graham cracker in the milk longer than anyone else without it falling apart.

2. Publishing: What happened? How comfortable were you in taking risks?

3. Processing: How are risks and rewards related?

4. Generalizing: What could you have done to be more successful in taking risks in this activity?

5. Applying: What does this activity suggest that you might want to do when you return to your workplace?

The "Graham Cracker Challenge" was previously published in *The 2013 Pfeiffer Training Annual,* John Goldberg, contributor; Elaine Biech, editor.

83 Experiential Learning on the Job

_____ **Overview** _____

A strategy that takes learners to the learning experience in a real way.

Participants

Up to 25 individuals who can travel to the learning site

Procedure

1. Determine what knowledge and skills are most important. Next, determine what experience would supply that transfer of knowledge and skills. Make that the focus of the learning instead of building simulations or a PowerPoint slide presentation.

2. Look at that experience as a complete picture. What happens just before and what happens after the experience that you want your learners to have? Be sure that you have included enough of the "brackets" on either side of the event to ensure a holistic experience.

3. Finally, hold a debriefing of the experience and tie it all back to the purpose of the activity.

Variation

A simulation or game can be built if time and cost make it impossible for participants to travel to the learning location.

Case Example

A large, packaged food manufacturing company wanted to give their up-and-coming leaders an opportunity to experience the company from a holistic perspective. The challenge was to help new leaders develop a strategic understanding of the business. The experiential event started with a farm tour;

most of the participants had never been on a farm. After viewing the raw agricultural products, the next experience was to tour a plant in order to appreciate the processes and capabilities of the company. The third experience was a shopper immersion exercise, in which leaders were given a set amount of money, a defined scenario, and a shopping list to purchase food for their families. Finally, the closing experience was a cooking activity to celebrate the end of the event.

You can read the entire story in detail in the *ASTD Handbook: The Definitive Reference for Training and Development* (ATD Press, 2014), in which Kris Zilliox relates the experience of designing this exciting experiential event.

84 Experiential Blended Learning for High Potentials

Overview

This blended-approach strategy presents future leaders with a way to learn about themselves and then practice their skills, which require them to improve on a real project, with feedback.

Participants

A group of high-potential employees

Procedure

1. High-potential (often referred to as "HIPO") employees are critical to your organization's future. Selecting them is the first step.

2. In this strategy, provide a group of high-potential learners with feedback in the form of 360-degree instruments. Hold the session off-site and ensure confidentiality. Learners return to the organization with a list of skills they need to improve.

3. The entire group selects a project that they will complete as a team. The project adds value to the organization.

4. Facilitators from the office of the talent manager provide feedback and coaching to the learners throughout the project about teamwork, leadership, communication, and other skills that need to be developed.

Variation

This strategy could be used with any group. It is very effective.

Case Example

A leadership development program for a research client is needed to support their high-potential future leaders. The organization opens the application process each year, and about 50 percent of all applicants are selected to create a new "class." The candidates attend an off-site leadership development program at the Center for Creative Leadership (CCL) as a first step, where they obtain comprehensive feedback on their strengths and needs. Within six months of initiation, each new class must select a project and complete it as a team. The planning and design is done in a classroom setting, but some parts (depending upon the project) are done outside the classroom.

Examples of experiential projects for past classes included the following. One class created the organization's first business plan that was implemented by leadership. Another class chose to create a video that will be shown to high school students and on kiosks provided by STEM's (Science, Technology, Engineering, Math) effort to encourage students to pursue science and technology careers. Throughout the project, facilitated discussions address what participants are learning about themselves, leadership, and teamwork. In addition, participants are expected to maintain a journal of their experiences and their personal learning goals.

On-the-Job Assignments

Developing employees is "job one," to paraphrase an American carmaker. And that "job one" belongs to supervisors. Supervisors have many tools at their disposal; rotational assignments, stretch assignments, project-based assignments, and others. Supervisors decide which learning strategies and developmental assignments will be most beneficial for all employees. Supervisors should consider what each employee needs to know and what developmental assignments are beneficial to both the employee and the organization. Supervisors should then tap into a variety of options in order to provide employees with those assignments. This section addresses temporary assignments that are available for developmental purposes.

85   Assessing Learners for a Rotational Assignment

_____ Overview _____

This strategy provides guidance for rotational assessment and selection.

Participants

1–15 depending on the setting

Procedure

1. Review the template in the Case Example and add or delete any content as necessary.

2. Define a rotational assignment to your learner(s). Halelly Azulay, author of *Employee Development on a Shoestring* (ASTD Press, 2012), defines a job rotation assignment as "a temporary assignment of an employee to a different job, usually laterally, in another role in the same organization, for an agreed upon time."

3. Distribute the template to your identified learners for the rotational program to complete on their own. The template will help them assess their own strengths and weaknesses.

4. Use the information to help determine an appropriate rotational opportunity for each learner.

Variations

- You could combine this assessment with an interview.
- You could work one-on-one with each learner to complete the assessment together.

Case Example

A fast-growing R&D company reviewed its candidates for promotion, and realized that it had a very young workforce that was not ready to be promoted.

After completing an assessment that was similar to the one in this activity, a group of promising employees were interviewed by three different leaders in the company. Once the high-potential candidate list was completed, a leadership development plan was created for each candidate. To ensure that targeted employees had a chance at being promoted, the talent manager established a rotational plan to provide opportunities for them to experience working in key departments. In addition, decisions were made about which employee needed specific skill focus based on the assessment. Special developmental assignments paired with course work were provided.

Rotational Program Self-Assessment and Application

Name

Current Position/Title

Current Department

Tenure

♦ In Role

♦ Overall in organization

Educational experience

1. List three to four of your core strengths.

2. List three to four of your key development areas.

3. Rate yourself on a scale of 1–7 (1 = Needs significant development; 7 = Strength) and add a comment to explain your rating.

♦ Product Development

♦ Business Development

♦ Technology

♦ Operations

♦ Finance

(continued)

- Marketing
- Sales
- Customer Support
- Strategy
- Other

4. List four examples of how you display the organization's expected leadership skills and behaviors.

5. Discuss your career goals and the path you are interested in pursuing in 100–150 words.

6. In 400–500 words, discuss why you want to participate in the rotational program. What are your expectations? How will it benefit you and the organization?

7. Supervisor's comments (completed by candidate's supervisor).

Source: ebb associates inc.

86 Department Rotation Agreements

Overview

This strategy provides leaders with an interdepartment agreement for an employee exchange.

Participants

Usually one learner plus representatives from the two participating departments

Procedure

1. Even though rotational assignments can be a great developmental opportunity for individual learners, departments may not be excited to either "lose one of our best employees" or "have the added responsibility to develop an additional employee." Therefore, an important step in initiating rotational assignments is to have a clear working agreement between the two departments.

2. Although logically the employee does not need to be involved, it is another developmental opportunity you can provide for employees, allowing them to be a part of—or at least to observe—the negotiation of details for a rotational assignment.

3. The template should be revised to meet your organizational needs. Use it to guide a meeting between the two departments.

Variation

This formal agreements may not be needed in your organization. Agreements can be made with a handshake.

Case Example

An already thinly stretched contracts shop in a small state agency was dismayed when their star contract specialist was encouraged to accept and finally did accept a year-long rotation to the finance department. After a year, the employee returned to his original position as a contract specialist. He was appreciative of his department head allowing him to have an extraordinary learning experience when he knew the department was already short staffed. The employee brought back information from the finance department and was excited to share what he had learned with his colleagues. What he taught others made their jobs easier when they needed to work with the finance department. The department head was pleased with not only what the employee learned but also with his confidence and new ability to be more decisive. Given this, the employee was promoted to a supervisory position as soon as an opening was available.

Rotational Assignment Agreement between (Department A) and (Department B)

Subject: Rotational Assignment Number _____ for (Employee).

Purpose: This agreement establishes objectives, responsibilities, conditions, and/or special procedures regarding the assignment.

Objectives: Describe rotational assignment objectives.

Responsibilities: Describe who is responsible for what, for example, salary, travel, performance appraisal, time cards, vacation time, training, evaluation of assignments, and others.

Considerations: Describe any additional procedures, provisions, or conditions, such as coordination between home and host offices; conditions/process for early termination of the assignment; or other concerns.

Unless specified otherwise, the participant will return to his or her position of record at the conclusion of the assignment.

Effective Date:

Duration: _____

Current Supervisor (Name, Title, Date, Phone)

Host Supervisor (Name, Title, Date, Phone)

Source: ebb associates inc.

87 Evaluating Rotational Assignments

Overview

This strategy provides the learner with a way to evaluate his or her progress and results for a rotational assignment.

Participants

Usually one

Procedure

1. This process starts with the beginning of a rotational assignment and ends when the rotational assignment ends.

2. Meet with your learner before the individual leaves for the rotational assignment in order to identify objectives for involvement in the program. Use the application that the learner completes as a resource. The learner should do most of the work, with your guidance to push a bit or to offer ideas where necessary. The goal should be to ensure that the learner gains skills and knowledge, has an experience that stretches the learner's current skills, and shapes an attitude of continuous learning.

3. A sample format is displayed in the Case Example.

4. From experience, this works best when you schedule two to four separate meetings of 30–45 minutes' duration for each, separated by a day or two to complete the document with meaningful objectives.

5. When the learner returns from the rotational assignment, use the document and objectives that the learner completed prior to the rotational assignment. What objectives were achieved (why not if they weren't)? What does the learner want to apply on the job as a result of the rotational assignment? What are the learner's next steps for development?

Variation

Sometimes a similar result can occur if the employee takes on a project within the department or leads a cross-functional team as an additional responsibility.

Case Example

Rotational Assignment Goals

Planning

List five objectives that you wish to accomplish on this rotational assignment.

What specific skills do you intend to acquire or improve?

What knowledge do you plan to acquire?

How will you receive feedback?

What coaching or mentoring do you desire, and how do you plan to receive it?

What experiences will be beneficial to you and the organization? Provide a rationale.

What unique opportunities should be included in this assignment?

How will you record and report your progress?

What measures will you use to assess your success?

Do you have any other comments?

On Assignment Tracking

How I am tracking what I am learning

Decisions I made that were wise

Decisions I made that needed more thought and what I learned from them

Milestones that changed; why they changed; how they changed; the result

One-quarter into the assignment
Halfway through the assignment

How I rate accomplishment of:

Objectives

Skills

Knowledge

Experiences

How I sum up the results of my assignment

How I evaluate the experiences

Source: ebb associates inc.

88   Stretch Assignment: Yes or No?

_____ Overview _____

This tool provides you and your employee an opportunity to evaluate whether the employee is ready for a stretch assignment.

Participants

Usually one

Procedure

1. Generally, this situation will occur when your organization has a requirement that doesn't fit into anyone's job description or when no one is available to take on any additional responsibility. There may be a requirement for someone to lead a team, implement a new project, serve on a team, act as a representative on a governing or industrial body, turn a failing operation around, or some other need. Perhaps your department has been asked to provide an employee for a particular cause. You may have one or more employees who are potential future leaders. A stretch assignment can help you evaluate their potential, give them a developmental opportunity, and, in many cases, put them in front of others in the organization.

2. Define a "stretch assignment" to your employee as a task or a project that is a "stretch" beyond the employee's current job description, which will challenge the employee. Explain that you would like to discuss the possibility of this opportunity with the employee but that you would first like the employee to evaluate his or her readiness for the opportunity.

3. Provide the "Stretch Assignment Readiness Self-Assessment" to the employee(s) to complete. Meet with each one to discuss the employee's readiness and next steps. If the employee is ready, what are the next preparation steps toward the stretch assignment? If the employee is not ready, what can the individual do to get ready?

4. Scoring: If the employee's responses tend to fall more to the left side of the spectrum (between "Not really ready" and "Somewhat ready"), the individual may be a good candidate for a stretch assignment. The current role does not present sufficient challenges and opportunities to grow. If the employee's responses tend to fall more to the right of the spectrum (between "Somewhat ready" and "Definitely ready"), the employee is sufficiently challenged and is probably not ready for a stretch assignment in the current role.

Variation

You could utilize recent feedback from a 360-degree feedback instrument to determine an employee's readiness for a stretch assignment.

Case Example

A branch manager for a midwestern bank realized that he would lose one of his best people in the loan department if he did not provide new opportunities for her. About the same time, the vice president requested someone from the branch to work on a taskforce to update the corporate strategy. The branch manager decided that it was more than serendipitous and asked his employee to complete the self-assessment found in Halelly Azulay's book. After she completed it, the branch manager told her what was happening and reviewed the results of the assessment with her. Other than "having to work with difficult people," the employee was a positive choice for a stretch assignment. She had never been involved in anything like this before. She asked for recommendations for books she could read to get up to speed and headed happily to her new assignment.

Stretch Assignment Readiness Self-Assessment

Consider your current job and rate yourself using the following assessment.

The coming year will bring significant changes.

Not really   Somewhat   Definitely

I will be exposed to critical new skills in my current job.

Not really   Somewhat   Definitely

My team's work and my work will significantly impact the success of the organization.

Not really   Somewhat   Definitely

The current job allows me to work closely with senior leaders and/or the board of directors of the organization.

Not really   Somewhat   Definitely

My successes or failures are highly visible in this job assignment.

Not really   Somewhat   Definitely

I am held responsible if the team doesn't accomplish its goals.

Not really   Somewhat   Definitely

I am pushed to the edge of my comfort zone in the current job.

Not really   Somewhat   Definitely

I am faced with significant never-before-experienced challenges in areas that are important for my development.

●——●

Not really   Somewhat   Definitely

My current job requires me to significantly expand my leadership capabilities.

●——●

Not really   Somewhat   Definitely

I have so much work that the only way I can get my work done on time is by making tough decisions to delegate tasks to others in order to get things done.

●——●

Not really   Somewhat   Definitely

I have to influence people and groups over whom I have no direct authority.

●——●

Not really   Somewhat   Definitely

I have to partner with multiple stakeholders who have different or competing agendas.

●——●

Not really   Somewhat   Definitely

I have to work with difficult people to get things done.

●——●

Not really   Somewhat   Definitely

Reprinted by permission from Halelly Azulay, *Employee Development on a Shoestring* (Alexandria, VA: ASTD Press, 2012), 100.

Learning beyond the Workplace

Learning Outside the Organization

Learning doesn't stop when you leave work. Rather, it may just begin. You have teaching options, books to read, association meetings to attend, and people to meet. There are endless things you can do and learn as long as you keep your eyes open and your options moving forward. Learn customer service at the local theme park? Learn feedback skills by coaching a youth sports team? Learn followership during a scuba excursion? Learn leadership skills by serving as a civic league president? Learn risk taking by skydiving? All are possible. Start your list today.

89   Teach a Class

_____ **Overview** _____

A strategy to help someone gain practice in public speaking.

Participants

Anyone

Procedure

1. The best way to practice public speaking is to do it.

2. Help a learner find a place where the skills can be practiced outside the organization. There will be other benefits as well.

3. Start with these suggestions:

+ Local community colleges are always looking for someone to teach a class, such as coin collecting, genealogy, golf, or whatever the learner's hobby happens to be.

+ High schools welcome people who are willing to come in to talk about their careers. Contact school counselors or high school business education departments.

+ Local youth organizations or clubs, such as the pony club, 4-H, Junior Achievement, YPO, Big Brothers/Sisters, Young Entrepreneurs, and others also welcome people who are willing to come in to talk about a variety of topics.

4. Once a learner gains experience outside the organization, a natural next step is to deliver a presentation about the experience.

Variation

A learner could run for office in an organization. It could be a professional organization, hobby group, reading club, sports club, civic organization, charity group—whatever resonates with the learner. All officers need to speak up at meetings to deliver reports.

Case Example

A wholesale manufacturing representative wanted to be a leader in his organization. Although he belonged to the debate team in college, he disliked every moment of it. He knew to accomplish his dream of being a leader required him to be more comfortable and skilled as a speaker. He joined the local chamber of commerce as a representative for his organization. When they were looking for individuals to provide leadership and team skills to youth in the city, he begrudgingly volunteered. He was successful in starting the program. To establish the program, he networked with organizations around the world, including EmprendeAhora.

EmprendeAhora is a leadership and entrepreneurship training program giving university students from rural Peru the necessary tools and empowerment to open their own businesses, generate income, and create local employment. The program trains the best university students from all over Peru in leadership, democracy, market economy, and business planning. EmprendeAhora lasts for three to five months (90 classroom hours), and the program is divided into three sessions consisting of classes; business plan coaching; lectures by successful entrepreneurs, leading academics, and political leaders; educational trips to large companies; and workshops led by young leaders from Lima. To graduate and receive a certificate, students are required to organize their own leadership and entrepreneurial workshops in their communities for high school or university students in order to share their knowledge and values from the program. Another requirement for completing the EmprendeAhora program is creating a business plan.

The manufacturing representative taught classes, coached students, and led workshops, all of which gave him many options for public speaking in Peru and in his hometown.

90   Do You Belong?

Overview

A strategy that taps into the fabulous resource that associations provide for employee development.

Participants

All learners

Procedure

1. Encourage learners to join an appropriate professional association.

2. Discuss how membership in the association will become a resource for skills and knowledge. Encourage the learners to attend local meetings and conferences.

3. Ask them about what they have read in the association's publications and how they use the association's website. If they get involved, it is a guaranteed way to learn and grow.

4. The learners will meet people with whom to network. If the association doesn't have the answer to a question, the new network of professionals will be able to lead the learners in the right direction. Joining an association is an opportunity for learners to affect their own destiny and to invest in themselves.

Variation

There are no substitutes for joining a professional association. However, if you must consider a variation, learners could subscribe to industry or professional association publications in order to keep up with what is happening in the industry.

Case Example

A trainer, new to the profession, attended her first national conference for ATD (Association for Talent Development). She was astounded at all the resources available and the thousands of things she did not know about the profession. She knew her learning had just begun.

91   The Envelope, Please

Overview

A strategy that takes a learner out of the world of work to analyze movies and compare what makes a good movie with what makes doing a good job at anything.

Participants

Anyone

Procedure

1. There are many ways to decide which are the top movies of all time: by genre, by highest earnings, by vote. Listed in the Case Example are the top movies based on the number of Oscars they won.

2. Give the learner a copy of the Academy Awards nominations and winners. Suggest that the learner rent one of these movies and decide what made it the best. How did the directors, producers, and cast achieve what they did?

3. Suggest that the learners compare what they do on the job with what the cast and production crew do to reach Academy Award status. What could the learner do differently to reach Academy Award status?

Variation

A similar comparison could be made with the learner's favorite sports team, a Nobel prize winner, or a design or building project.

Case Example

Academy Award–Winning Movies

Movie	Year	Nominations	Awards
Ben-Hur	1959	12	11
Titanic	1997	14	11
The Lord of the Rings: The Return of the King	2003	11	11
West Side Story	1961	11	10
Gigi	1958	9	9
The Last Emperor	1987	9	9
The English Patient	1996	12	9
Gone with the Wind	1939	13	8
From Here to Eternity	1953	13	8
On the Waterfront	1954	12	8
My Fair Lady	1964	12	8
Cabaret	1972	10	8
Gandhi	1982	11	8
Amadeus	1984	11	8
Slumdog Millionaire	2008	10	8

92   Google Your Company

Overview

A strategy that will help employees see their company from the public's perspective and determine what they can do to improve its status.

Participants

Anyone

Procedure

1. Use Google or some other search engine to learn more about the organization where the learner works.

2. Have the learner search the company's name on the Internet and then respond to questions such as the following:

   ◆ What did you learn about the company?

   ◆ What surprised you about the company?

   ◆ What is the reputation of the company?

   ◆ What did you learn about the company that helps you understand what is driving its business?

   ◆ What did you learn about the company that influences your next steps?

3. Ask the learner to create a plan that addresses anything that was uncovered that needs correcting or changing.

Variation

If your company is local, search the local newspaper's archives if they are not available on Google.

Case Example

One October a state forest ranger searched online for the parks at which he worked. He was surprised to see the negative comments over the past summer about a lack of places to put garbage. When he checked with his boss, he found that the agency knew there was a problem but no one had time to address it during the summer months. He asked his boss if he could take this on as a special project and put a plan in place for the following summer.

93   Visit the City Council

_____ Overview _____

Use this strategy to learn how to think about the big picture by considering how local government affairs may affect the business or the industry.

Participants

Anyone

Procedure

1. Staying current on city, state, and federal government affairs and how they may affect the industry and the impact they may have on the business is more important the higher up the corporate ladder a learner climbs. It is never too soon to start.

2. Suggest that a learner invite a friend who works in a different company, and perhaps even a different industry, to attend a city council meeting with you.

3. After the meeting ends, the learner can suggest that they stop for a beverage and discuss the implications of the decisions that are in process for your city.

4. Ask the learner after the council meeting what implications the learner saw that could affect either the company or the industry. Note that even something like building a new school that doesn't appear on the surface to affect the business, most likely will. A bond referendum may need to occur, property taxes may increase, or the sales tax may increase. All of these affect the business and its customers.

Variations

• Instead of visiting a city council meeting, the learner could simply review past council meeting notes.

• A visit to a state or federal lawmakers' meeting could be substituted.

Case Example

A woman who worked in the claims department of an insurance company head-quartered in the woman's state capital took this exact advice. Two years later, she ran for a position on the school board. Her school board experience was a dynamic and exciting learning experience.

94   Read a Biography

_____ **Overview** _____

A strategy for reading about a great leader and gleaning ideas for personal development.

Participants

Anyone

Procedure

1. Using the best biography list given below or your own recommendations, select a book.

2. Study the book for what you can learn about the leader and use what you learn in your life by asking questions such as the following:

- What do you value the most about this person's life?
- What is the person's most admirable quality?
- What was the most surprising thing you learned about this person?
- How has this book inspired you to do something differently?

Variation

Select your favorite person from history or business and read a book by or about this individual.

Case Example

Here is a list of several biographies and autobiographies that are mentioned on many lists, in no particular order:

- *Malice Toward None: Abraham Lincoln,* by Jack E. Levin
- *Churchill: A Life,* by Martin Gilbert

- *Unbroken*, by Laura Hillenbrand
- *Killing Patton*, by Bill O'Reilly
- *Steve Jobs*, by Walter Isaacson
- *Mandela's Way*, by Richard Stengel
- *The Clinton Charisma*, by Donald Phillips
- *A Portrait of My Father*, by George W. Bush
- *The Oprah Phenomenon*, by Jennifer Harris
- *Ben Franklin*, autobiography
- *Benjamin Franklin*, by Walter Isaacson
- *Richard Branson*, autobiography
- *Helen Keller*, by Leslie Garrett
- *Gandhi*, by Primo Levi
- *Gandhi An Autobiography: The Story of My Experiments with Truth*, autobiography
- *Amelia Earhart*, by Tanya Lee Stone
- *Thomas Edison*, by Matthew Josephson
- *Mother Teresa*, by Kathryn Spink
- *Martin Luther King, Jr.*, by Marshall Frady
- *Eleanor Roosevelt*, autobiography
- *John F. Kennedy: An Unfinished Life*, by Robert Dallek
- *Thomas Jefferson*, by Jon Meacham
- *His Excellency: George Washington*, by Joseph Ellis

95   Visit Your Supplier

_____ Overview _____

A strategy that helps employees understand the supplier end of their business.

Participants

Small group of people who have ties to the organization's suppliers

Procedure

1. Depending upon your position, you may need to discuss this learning activity with someone in senior leadership prior to scheduling the activity. Have a small group plan to meet with a key supplier. The purpose is to learn more about the organizational drivers that are affecting your supplier today or that they anticipate will affect your supplier in the future. External drivers may include economic, customer, market, regulations, public perception, or human resources. Internal business drivers may include systems changes, technology, shareholder, financial, leadership, structure, or cultural shift.

2. Create a list of questions such as these to initiate the discussion:

   - What are the key drivers that are affecting your strategy today?

   - What drivers are you concerned about in the future?

   - How critical are these differences?

   - What impact will these differences have on you?

   - What impact might they have on us as one of your customers? What can we expect?

   - How can we help you? What role do you want us to play?

3. Summarize your discussion and share your discussion with your supervisor.

Variations

- Invite your supplier to your organization.
- Request a tour of your supplier's plant.

Case Example

A small group of employees from a clothing retailer that specializes in casual clothes visited suppliers of the cotton that is used in its clothing. These suppliers are special; they supply the cotton used in clothing made with "Supima" cotton. Supima cotton is grown exclusively in the United States. Only the top 3 percent of America's cotton crop earns Supima status. The name "Supima" is a contraction of "Superior Pima." It was coined in 1954 by American growers who wanted to safeguard the quality and reputation of pima cotton. Because it takes a hot climate with limited moisture to yield the fibers, Supima cotton is supplied by only about 500 growers in California, Arizona, New Mexico, and Texas. The group of employees wanted to learn more about the process of growing this unique cotton and to learn if the growers were concerned about weather or pests that might harm production. They also wanted to learn how they could strengthen their relationship with the suppliers.

96 Office Hours II

Overview

This strategy redefines the "open-door policy" to extend time to talk to a supervisor in a setting that allows more candor.

Participants

Anyone

Procedure

1. Create a personalized way to meet with your employees more often. Finding a way to do this outside the office encourages a greater flow of conversation.

2. Typical opportunities are breakfast before the start of the workday or after work, perhaps establishing the meeting one to two hours prior to the end of the day.

3. If "office hours" will be held in the afternoon, announce the plan in the morning of the same day. If you plan a morning meeting, invite everyone the day prior to "office hours."

Variation

If you have virtual employees, invite them along, too—virtually. They can go to a different restaurant for breakfast and either call or Skype your organization.

Case Example

Scott is the director of corporate strategic communications. At least twice a month he announces that he will have office hours at a specific place at 3:00 p.m. or so. The location is within walking distance and always the same to keep things simple. His employees know this is a time for both catching up on what others are doing in the department as well as to hear the "inside scoop" about the company.

Do Well by Doing Good

Providing time and talent by volunteering is a way to learn and give something back at the same time. Volunteering comes in all roles and sizes. Volunteers may have skills that they share with others, or it may be a learning experience for them. Volunteering may occur within the same skill set and profession or be something completely different. Someone in marketing may volunteer to assist the local food bank to create marketing copy for the upcoming holidays, or an accountant may volunteer to help small business owners. On the other hand, a scientist may volunteer to lead a team to build a playground for an inner city park, gaining team leadership skills. Employees who volunteer almost always learn skills, such as leadership, communication, and teamwork. They can target specific skills, such as improving their budgeting or marketing skills. But they gain many other benefits as well. Often there is an increase in cultural awareness or in seeing issues from a different perspective. They learn how to problem solve and make contacts with others outside their typical circle of people. And, of course, there is always the value of giving back to society.

97 Volunteer Team Needs a Leader

_____ Overview _____

A strategy for participants to gain leadership skills while volunteering.

Participants

A department or select group of individuals in a department

Procedure

1. Identify several opportunities for volunteering in the community that could benefit from a team effort. Here are several suggestions:

   - One-time community service team, such as a spring neighborhood clean-up day or serving in a soup kitchen.

   - Emergency disaster relief, such as holding a yard sale to raise money for families who were in a local fire or flood.

   - Support for a local event, such as building a float for the local Thanksgiving Day parade or sponsoring a team in a "fun run" or parking cars.

   - Support for other volunteer efforts, such as youth going to another state or country to provide aid or assistance.

2. Identify individuals who need to practice leadership and teamwork skills. Invite each of them to lead a volunteer team from work to participate in one of the events.

3. After the event, review what happened. How was the event handled differently by the organizing group? What skills and learning would the individuals like to transfer to their department?

Variation

Present the idea, but let the employees also locate the volunteer opportunities.

Case Example

An employee joined forces with a high school to sponsor a "pajama party" at a local big box store. The event took place after hours on a Friday night. The entry fee was one pair of new or gently used pajamas, which were donated to needy families in the area. The store ran fabulous specials for anyone who showed up in pajamas. The high school jazz band played music from 10 p.m. to midnight, and the parents association served free appetizers and lemonade. The sports boosters held a bake sale, and the cheerleaders and the football team served as hosts to help people locate items in the store. The volunteer employee learned how to coordinate volunteers, set goals, create schedules, and manage many details.

98   Professional Association Involvement

_____ Overview _____

A strategy that builds skills, delivers experience, and helps others through volunteering.

Participants

One or more

Procedure

1. Belonging to a professional organization is the best way to stay current in a field or industry. Helping your employees see this rationale is important for their development. Sometimes organizations pay the dues; sometimes they do not. This should not matter. Belonging to a professional organization is a way for individuals to validate themselves. Employees' ability to keep up with the profession depends on staying in touch.

2. Explain to employees that affiliation with a national professional association or group is critical to maintaining professional awareness. Engineers need to stay in touch with a field that is changing daily. Finance people and others need to maintain their certification. New employees need to see that a membership is an investment in themselves. If they don't invest in themselves, who will?

3. Joining is the first step. Getting involved is the second step. Encourage employees to find opportunities to do more than just write a check for the membership dues of an association. The networking has an unmeasurable return on the investment of time. They can volunteer to:

   ◆ Run for office

   ◆ Serve on a committee

   ◆ Help with a conference

- ◆ Present content at a meeting
- ◆ Mentor others new to the field

4. Encourage those who have successfully joined and volunteered to help a professional group to share what they gain with others.

Variation

Your organization could host a professional organization's meeting. Accompany the meeting with a corporate tour or sharing of information about your organization that would be of interest to the group. For example, if you just reconfigured the office space to be more collaborative, share the design and the rationale with the group.

Case Example

A trainer new to the Association of Talent Development (ATD) attended her first chapter meeting, where she was approached to volunteer to write a newsletter article about the project she described when she was introduced to the group. (Volunteers are few, so this is common.) Three meetings later, she was assisting the newsletter editor with the blog. Today, she is a published author, saying she never would have known how much she liked writing if it were not for that ATD experience.

99 Find a Match

_____ Overview _____

A volunteering option that taps into an individual's need for growth and development.

Participants

Learners who need to shore up their skills when there is no apparent option within their organization

Procedure

1. You may have a learner who needs a general development experience, an opportunity to learn in a different setting, or has a specific skill that needs developing. A Deloitte Volunteer IMPACT Survey stated that 86 percent of employed Americans believe that volunteering had a positive impact on their careers. Skills specified included:

   ◆ Leadership: 93 percent

   ◆ Problem solving: 89 percent

   ◆ Decision making: 88 percent

   ◆ Negotiating: 82 percent

2. Determine the purpose of the developmental option and share the idea with the learner. Help the learner identify a nonprofit or volunteer group in the area that may be able to provide what is needed.

3. Meet with the leader of the nonprofit group and outline what the volunteer can contribute and what kinds of experiences the learner needs. If it appears to be a match, turn the process over to the leader of the nonprofit group and the learner to work out the details.

Variation

The learner could be expected to locate his or her own organization. This is a learning experience in itself.

Case Example

A new consultant wanted an opportunity to practice team-building skills. She wrote a proposal and shared it with the local technical college, which she knew had a limited budget. The proposal was accepted, and a one-day team-building activity ensued. The technical college president was satisfied with the results. Ten years later, the consultant looks back on the experience as a great opportunity for learning what to do and what *not* to do!

100 Adopt a Group

An opportunity for a group of employees to establish a long-term relationship and hone a variety of skills while doing good at the same time.

Participants

A department or select group of employees who want to hone their skills and make a contribution to the community

Procedure

1. This active learning event probably needs to be sanctioned by senior management.

2. Identify a nonprofit or volunteer group in your company's area that helps others or helps to create a better community in some way.

3. Establish a relationship that addresses the purpose of the relationship. Create a memorandum of understanding (MOU) that establishes the parameters. See the case example for potential questions that can be covered.

4. Create ownership in the group regarding who manages this developmental opportunity.

5. Work with the nonprofit group to devise a useful onboarding experience for the volunteers and a team-building session to bring the two groups together.

6. One of the beauties of this strategy is that a group of volunteers has a variety of needs and skills, ensuring that it is a win-win situation for both the nonprofit group and the employees.

   ♦ Examples of what the corporate volunteers can achieve:
   Gain a fresh perspective of similar problems
   Increase cultural awareness
   Opportunity to try out new skills
   Increase network

   ◆   Examples of what the corporate volunteers can provide to the nonprofit group:

       Expertise and leadership

       A different perspective

       An entrepreneurial viewpoint

       Experience

Variation

Create and support a scholarship fund to help those in the nonprofit group or those served by the nonprofit group so that they can obtain an educational experience.

Case Example

A volunteer MOU between a company and a nonprofit group should discuss the following:

- The purpose of the MOU
- Desired outcomes and how they will be measured
- Obligations of each party
- Roles and responsibilities
- Resources required
- Communication plan
- Liability
- Terms and renewability
- Severability
- A clear description of the purpose and what can be expected from each other
- Signatures

101   Internal Fund-Raising

Overview

This strategy provides an opportunity for inexperienced employees to learn skills as they work beside a senior leader.

Participants

One or two rising stars in an organization who need practical experiences

Procedure

1. Most organizations support the community in numerous ways through loaned executives or internal fund-raising led by a corporate executive.

2. This is a great short-term opportunity to assign one or two rising stars in the organization who need to be exposed to senior leaders and who need opportunities to experience unique developmental opportunities.

3. The advantages are obvious:

   - The employees gain job enrichment and see work from a different perspective.

   - The executive has a couple of people who he or she can depend on to help with some of the details.

Variation

This could be tied to a continuing development opportunity in which the employees continue to work with the agency for a short time after the official experience has been completed.

Case Example

A vice president of an insurance company led the city's effort to raise funds for the United Way Campaign. He invited three people to attend planning meetings with him for the four-month time period. The following year, each of the three people led the campaign in their departments, although they were the most junior employees to have ever had those responsibilities.

A Bonus "10 Tips" List

10 Ways to Think about Learning in the Future

The future of learning is here now. The classroom is no longer bound by walls or calendar dates. CCL's (Center for Creative Leadership) concept of the Persistent Classroom™ embodies a learning future that is all around us—wherever our smartphone lies, whenever the time is right, and through whichever mode makes the most sense.

1. **The classroom is your GPS coordinates.** In the future, the classroom will not be a "place" but a coinhabited virtual space. It will not be bound by a date or specific physical space. Learning will be synchronous and asynchronous, local and distant, with each learner engaging though a multiplicity of digital portals. Learners will not come to a classroom; the classroom will come to them.

2. **Virtual learning spaces and digital hallways.** In the future, there will no longer be a distinction between what is analog and what is digital, or between concrete and virtual leaning spaces. All learning will occur within an "augmented reality" paradigm, and learners will receive a continuous stream of data that can be queried about people, places, and objects as they interact with the world.

3. **It's about presence.** The smartphone will yield to the personal heads-up display, which in turn will yield to the "chipped" person. People will be instantly locatable, and the acquisition of knowledge will occur just-in-time.

4. **Becoming digitally literate.** To be successful, trainers of the future will need to transcend physicality and develop a fully rendered digital identification, becoming diligent participants of emerging modes of radical connectivity.

5. **Radical connectivity and continuous learning.** Learning spaces in the future will be "always on." Everyone will be connected regardless of physical location. We will learn together, but we will be physically apart. We will learn by multiplying and intensifying our connections.

6. **Becoming sensitive to nonvisual signs.** Learning is a process of becoming sensitive to signs and events—how to both be affected by them and to affect them. To be successful in the future, trainers must recalibrate their senses to create meaning associated with signs inherent in a world of words without sight and even sound.

7. **Crowd sourcing knowledge.** In the future, instructors/trainers will be only one source of knowledge. When learners inhabit a radically connected learning space, expert knowledge holders (and what they know) are both student and teacher…and are just a click away.

8. **Think snacks, not meals.** When designing a curriculum, content should be broken into a series of "bite-sized" pieces. Traditional location-based instructional design needs to be reimagined for unwalled learning spaces, where learners drop in and out of the content stream.

9. **Gamification is not a game.** Incorporating game mechanics and game design techniques to engage and motivate people to achieve their learning goals will be the standard in instructional design.

10. **Learner-curated education and the democratization of learning.** In the future, people will inhabit a personally curated educational world where the curriculum is designed, moment-to-moment, by the participant. Instructional designers and trainers will work in a world where participants have equal agency as the trainer.

Ideas from David Powell, Center for Creative Leadership.

ADDITIONAL READING

Axelrod, Wendy and Coyle, Jeannie. *Make Talent Your Business: How Exceptional Managers Develop People While Getting Results*. San Francisco: Berrett-Koehler, 2011.

Azulay, H. "Assessing Readiness for a Mentoring Partnership," In E. Biech (ed.), *The Pfeiffer Annual: Training*. San Francisco: Wiley 2013.

Barbazette, J. *How to Write Terrific Training Materials: Methods, Tools, and Techniques*. San Francisco: Pfeiffer, 2013.

Betof, E. *Leaders as Teachers*. Alexandria, VA: ASTD Press, 2014.

Biech, E. *ASTD Handbook: The Definitive Reference for Training and Development*. Alexandria, VA: ASTD Press, 2008.

———. *The ASTD Handbook for Workplace Learning Professionals*. Alexandria, VA: ASTD Press, 2014.

Bozarth, J. *Social Media for Trainers*. San Francisco: Wiley, 2010.

Christopher, D. *The Successful Virtual Classroom*. New York: AMACOM, 2015.

Clark, R. *Evidence-based Training Methods*. Alexandria, VA: ASTD Press, 2014.

Huggett, C. *The Virtual Training Guidebook: How to Design, Deliver, and Implement Live Online Learning*. Alexandria, VA: ASTD Press, 2013.

Kapp, K. *The Gamification of Learning and Instruction*. San Francisco: Pfeiffer, 2012.

Kaye, B. *Love 'em or Lose 'em: Getting Good People to Stay*. San Francisco: Berrett-Koehler, 2012.

Labin, J. *Real-World Training Design*. Alexandria, VA: ASTD Press, 2012.

Maslow, A. *Toward a Psychology of Being*. New York: Litton Educational Publishing, 1968.

McCauley, C., DeRue, D., Yost, P., and Taylor, S. *Experience-Driven Leader Development*. San Francisco: Wiley, 2014.

Scisco, P., McCauley, C., Leslie, J., and Elsey R. *Change Now! Five Steps to Better Leadership*. Greensboro, NC: Center for Creative Leadership, 2014.

Stolovich, H., and Keeps, E. *Telling Ain't Training*. Alexandria, VA: ASTD Press, 2011.

Straining, L. *111 Creative Ways to use QR Codes*. USA: Learniappe Publishing, 2012.

"Volunteering Promotes Goodwill, Fosters Employee Development" August 01, 2005, http://hr.blr .com/HR-news/Staffing-Training/Employee-Manager-Training/Volunteering-Promotes-Goodwill-Fosters-Employee-De/

Watkins, R. *75 E-learning Activities: Making Online Courses More Interactive*. San Francisco: Jossey Bass/Wiley, 2005.

Wick, C., Pollock, R., Jefferson, A., and Flanagan, R. *The Six Disciplines of Breakthrough Learning*. San Francisco: Pfeiffer, 2010.

ABOUT THE AUTHOR

Elaine Biech, president of ebb associates inc, a strategic implementation, leadership development, and experiential learning consulting firm, has been in the field over 30 years helping organizations work through large-scale change. She has presented at dozens of national and international conferences and has been featured in such publications as *The Wall Street Journal, Harvard Management Update, Investor's Business Daily,* and *Fortune Magazine.* She is the author and editor of over 60 books, receiving national awards for 2 of them.

Several of her recent publications include: *The ASTD Handbook: The Definitive Reference for Training and Development, 2014; Developing Talent for Organizational Results,* 2012; *The Book of Road-Tested Activities,* 2011; *A Coach's Guide to Exemplary Leaders,* 2010; *ASTD Leadership Handbook,* 2010; *The Leadership Challenge Activities Book,* 2010; *ASTD's Ultimate Train the Trainer,* 2009; *10 Steps to Successful Training,* 2009; *The Consultant's Quick Start Guide, 2nd ed.,* 2009; *ASTD Handbook for Workplace Learning Professionals,* 2008; *Trainer's Warehouse Book of Games,* 2008; *The Business of Consulting, 2nd ed.,* 2007; *Thriving Through Change: A Leader's Practical Guide to Change Mastery,* 2007; *Successful Team-Building Tools, 2nd ed.,* 2007; *90 World-Class Activities by 90 World-Class Trainers,* 2007; *Training for Dummies,* 2005; *Marketing Your Consulting Services,* 2003; *The Consultant's Legal Guide,* 2000; *The Pfeiffer Annual for Consultants* and *The Pfeiffer Annual for Trainers* (1998–2013).

Elaine specializes in helping leaders maximize their effectiveness. Customizing all of her work for individual clients, she conducts strategic planning sessions and implements corporate-wide systems such as quality improvement, change management, reengineering of business processes, and mentoring programs. She facilitates topics such as coaching today's employees, fostering creativity, customer service, creating leadership development programs, time management, speaking skills, coaching, consulting skills, training competence, conducting productive meetings, managing corporate-wide change, handling the difficult employee, organizational communication, conflict resolution, and effective listening. She is particularly adept at turning dysfunctional teams into productive teams.

As a management consultant, trainer, and designer, Elaine has provided services globally to companies such as Outback Steakhouse, Johnson Wax, FAA, Land O' Lakes, McDonald's, Lands' End, General Casualty Insurance, Chrysler, Federal Reserve Bank, PricewaterhouseCoopers, China Sinopec, China Telecom, Banco de Credito Peru, Minera Yanacocha, Newmont Mining, American Family Insurance, Hershey Chocolate, U.S. Navy, NASA, Newport News Shipbuilding, Kohler Company, ATD, American Red Cross, Association of Independent CPAs, the University of Wisconsin, The College of William and Mary, ODU, and hundreds of other public and private-sector organizations to prepare them for current challenges.

A long-time volunteer for the Association of Talent Development (ATD) (formerly ASTD), Elaine has served on ASTD's National Board of Directors, was the recipient of the 1992 ASTD Torch Award, the 2004 ASTD Volunteer Staff Partnership Award, the 2006 Gordon Bliss Memorial Award, and in 2012, the inaugural CPLP Fellow Program Honoree from the ASTD Certification Institute. She was instrumental in compiling and revising the CPLP study guides and has designed five ASTD Certificate Programs. She was the 1995 Wisconsin Women Entrepreneur's Mentor Award recipient, has served on the Independent Consultants Association's (ICA) Advisory Committee and on the Instructional Systems Association (ISA) board of directors. Elaine is currently a member of the Center for Creative Leadership's Board of Governors.